Praise for
Al Mohler

"From grade inflation to global calamities, Albert Mohler is a steady guide. From the psychological coddling of the American ego to the hollowing of the American conscience, Mohler is unremittingly clear-headed. From Nineveh to New Orleans, Mohler holds the mirror at a blazing forty-five-degree angle between heaven and earth. The burning light of divine wisdom illumines a hundred shadows of our human folly. And at the center of the blaze is the mighty cross of Jesus Christ defining the final meaning of everything. I thank God for Albert Mohler."

—JOHN PIPER, pastor for preaching and vision,
Bethlehem Baptist Church, Minneapolis, MN

"Al Mohler is a unique gift to the church. *Culture Shift* combines penetrating theological discernment and insightful cultural analysis with a passion to faithfully proclaim the gospel of Jesus Christ. I'm delighted that Al's wisdom is now available in this book. May it be the first of many."

—C. J. MAHANEY, Sovereign Grace Ministries

"We all know, as Dorothy said to Toto, that 'we are not in Kansas anymore.' But how to apply the deep truths of our Christian faith to a culture that seems to be trans-mogrifying before our very eyes, well, that's perhaps the most difficult question facing the church today. In this well-written book, Al Mohler surveys the landscape and offers insight and wisdom that helps us do just this. A manifesto for responsible Christian engagement!"

—TIMOTHY GEORGE, founding dean of Beeson Divinity School of Samford University and senior editor of *Christianity Today* for *Culture Shift*

"Thoughtful Christians seeking to engage the culture from a well-informed and thoroughly biblical perspective will find an impressive resource in this new work by R. Albert Mohler. *Culture Shift* is an outstanding contribution, which I heartily recommend."

—DAVID S. DOCKERY, president, Union University

"Dr. Albert Mohler brings his intellectual brilliance, moral wisdom, and theological insight together in a book that belongs on the shelf of anyone who is interested in both understanding the shifting sands of morality in our culture and how to deal with it. If you are in that category this is a must read."

—JAMES MERRITT, pastor of Cross Pointe Church, Duluth, GA, and host of Touching Lives media ministry for *Culture Shift*

DESIRE
AND
DECEIT

THE REAL COST OF THE
NEW SEXUAL TOLERANCE

R. ALBERT MOHLER JR.

MULTNOMAH
BOOKS

DESIRE AND DECEIT
PUBLISHED BY MULTNOMAH BOOKS
12265 Oracle Boulevard, Suite 200
Colorado Springs, Colorado 80921
A division of Random House Inc.

Scripture quotations are taken from the New American Standard Bible®. ©
Copyright The Lockman Foundation 1960, 1962, 1963, 1968, 1971, 1972,
1973, 1975, 1977, 1995. Used by permission. (www.Lockman.org).

ISBN 978-1-60142-766-3

Published in association with the literary agency of Wolgemuth & Associates Inc.

Published in the United States by WaterBrook Multnomah, an imprint of The
Doubleday Publishing Group, a division of Random House Inc., New York.

MULTNOMAH and its mountain colophon are registered trademarks of Random
House Inc.

Library of Congress Cataloging-in-Publication Data
Mohler, R. Albert, 1959–
    Desire and deceit / R. Albert Mohler.—1st ed.
        p. cm.
    ISBN 978-1-60142-766-3
    1. Sex—Religious aspects—Christianity. I. Title.
BT708.M63 2008
241'.66—dc22

                    2008010737

CONTENTS

Acknowledgments ix

Preface xi

1. **From Father to Son**
   J. R. R. Tolkien on Sex 1

2. **A New Look at Lust**
   A Secular View 11

3. **Another Look at Lust**
   The Christian View 19

4. **Pornography and the Integrity of Christian Marriage**
   The Challenge 27

5. **Pornography and the Integrity of Christian Marriage**
   The Calling. 35

6. **Homosexuality in Theological Perspective**
   The Roots of a Movement 43

7. **Homosexuality in Theological Perspective**
   The Hermeneutic of Legitimization. 51

8. **Homosexuality in Theological Perspective**
   A Biblical Worldview 63

9. **Homosexuality in Theological Perspective**
   Responding to the Challenge 75

10. **The End of Friendship**
    How Sexual Confusion Has Tainted
    Friendship Between Men 85

11. **After the Ball**
    Why the Homosexual Movement Has Won 95

12. **Alfred Kinsey**
    The Man as He Really Was 103

13. **Mourning Gay Culture**
    The Riddle of Andrew Sullivan 113

14. **Lesbians Raising Sons**
    Got a Problem with That? 125

15. **The Age of Polymorphous Perversity**
    A Revolution Fueled by Ideas 133

16. **The Age of Polymorphous Perversity**
    Seven Strategies for Revolution 143

17. **The Age of Polymorphous Perversity**
    Can Civilization Survive? 155

To
Mary Katherine Mohler
"Katie"
Wonderful daughter and friend.
She grabbed hold of my heart the moment of her birth
and has never let go.

ACKNOWLEDGMENTS

In a very real sense, no author is an island. I am deeply indebted to so many friends and colleagues who have helped me to think through these complex issues. I especially want to thank Dean Russell Moore and Professor Ken Magnuson of The Southern Baptist Theological Seminary. At different points, they, along with many others, have helped to sharpen my thoughts.

As always, I am deeply indebted to Greg Gilbert, Director of Research in my office, who has rendered inestimable assistance in getting this project ready for publication.

Finally, I especially want to express gratitude to my wife, Mary, and our children, Katie and Christopher. They have supported me at every turn and have taught me so much about life and love.

ACKNOWLEDGMENTS

PREFACE

Sexuality is now a major fact of public life in America and around much of the world. In one sense, this is hardly new. After all, sexuality is a major part of human existence—an unavoidably complex and potentially explosive dynamic of human life. But sexuality is now a *public* issue—front and center in some of the biggest and most contentious debates of our times.

Sex and sexuality now drive much of our advertising, entertainment, and the cultural scripts that citizens use in common conversation. The sexual revolution of the 1960s was, in retrospect, only a signal of what was to come. By the early years of the twenty-first century, issues of sexuality were seemingly unavoidable. Elementary school students are being introduced to "family diversity" curricula, and major newspapers report on the phenomena of sexual promiscuity in homes for the aged. There seems to be virtually no part of the culture that is not dealing with sexuality in one way or another—and often with significant controversy.

Christians have a special stake and stewardship in the midst of this confusion. In the first place, Christians know that sex is both *more* and *less* important than the culture of laissez-faire sexuality can understand. Unlike the naturalistic evolutionists, Christians believe that the realities of gender and sexuality are intentional gifts of the Creator, who gave these gifts to His human creatures as both a blessing and a responsibility. Unlike the postmodern relativists, Christians cannot accept the claim that all sexual standards are mere social constructs. We believe that the Creator alone has the right to reveal His intention and commands concerning our stewardship of these gifts. Unlike the marketing geniuses and advertising gurus, we do not believe that sexuality is intended as a ploy to get attention and to create consumer demand. Unlike the pandering producers of sexualized entertainment, we do not believe that sex is primarily about laugh lines and titillation. Unlike the sexual revolutionaries of recent decades, we do not believe that sexuality is the means of liberating the self from cultural oppression.

In other words, we believe that sex is less important than many would have us believe. Human existence is not, first and foremost, about sexual pleasure and the display of sexuality. There is much more to human life, fulfillment, and joy. Sex simply cannot deliver the promises made by our hypersexualized society.

On the other hand, sex is far *more* important than

a secular society can envision. After all, the Christian worldview reveals that sex, gender, and sexuality are ultimately all about the creature's purpose to glorify the Creator. This frame of reference transforms the entire question and leaves the creature asking this: how do I celebrate and live out my stewardship of my sexuality and my exercise of this gift so that the Creator is most glorified? Needless to say, this is not the question driving the confusion in our sex-saturated culture.

This book is an attempt to look at many of today's most controversial and troubling issues concerning sexuality from the perspective of biblical Christianity. Every one of us has a stake in this, and Christians are responsible for a special witness to the meaning of sex and sexuality.

And all this, we know, is not only about how we are to *think* about these issues, but how we are to live.

FROM FATHER TO SON

J. R. R. Tolkien on Sex

The astounding popularity of J. R. R. Tolkien and his writings, magnified many times over by the success of *The Lord of the Rings* films, has ensured that Tolkien's fantasy world of moral meaning stands as one of the great literary achievements of our times.

In some sense, Tolkien was a man born out of time. A philologist at heart, he was most at home in the world of ancient ages, even as he witnessed the barbarism and horrors of the twentieth century. Celebrated as a popular author, he was an eloquent witness to permanent truths. His popularity on university campuses, extending from his own day right up to the present, is a powerful indication of the fact that Tolkien's writings reach the hearts of the young and those looking for answers.

Even as Tolkien is celebrated as an author and literary figure, some of his most important messages were communicated by means of letters, and some of his most important letters were written to his sons.

Tolkien married his wife Edith in 1916, and the marriage was blessed with four children. Of the four, three were boys. John was born in 1917, Michael in 1920, and Christopher in 1924. Priscilla, the Tolkiens' only daughter, was born in 1929. Tolkien dearly loved his children, and he left a literary legacy in the form of letters.[1] Many of these letters were written to his sons, and these letters represent not only a prime example of literary quality but a treasure of Christian teaching on matters of manhood, marriage, and sex. Taken together, these letters constitute a priceless legacy, not only to the Tolkien boys, but to all those with whom the letters have been shared.

In 1941, Tolkien wrote a masterful letter to his son Michael, dealing with marriage and the realities of

---

1. J. R. R. Tolkien, *The Letters of J. R. R. Tolkien*, ed. Christopher Tolkien (Boston: Houghton Mifflin, 2000).

human sexuality. The letter reflects Tolkien's Christian worldview and his deep love for his sons and, at the same time, also acknowledges the powerful dangers inherent in unbridled sexuality.

"This is a fallen world," Tolkien chided. "The dislocation of sex-instinct is one of the chief symptoms of the Fall. The world has been 'going to the bad' all down the ages. The various social forms shift, and each new mode has its special dangers: but the 'hard spirit of concupiscence' has walked down every street, and sat leering in every house, since Adam fell." This acknowledgment of human sin and the inevitable results of the Fall stands in stark contrast to the humanistic optimism that was shared by so many throughout the twentieth century. Even when the horrors of two world wars, the Holocaust, and various other evils chastened the century's dawning optimism regarding human progress, the twentieth century gave evidence of an unshakable faith in sex and its liberating power. Tolkien would have none of this.

"The devil is endlessly ingenious, and sex is his favorite subject," Tolkien insisted. "He is as good every bit at catching you through generous romantic or tender motives, as through baser or more animal ones." Thus, Tolkien advised his young son, then twenty-one, that the sexual fantasies of the twentieth century were demonic lies, intended to ensnare human beings. Sex was a trap, Tolkien warned, because human beings are capable of almost infinite rationalization in terms of sexual motives. Romantic love is not sufficient as a justification for sex, Tolkien understood.

Taking the point further, Tolkien warned his son that "friendship" between a young man and a young woman, supposedly free from sexual desire, would not long remain untroubled by sexual attraction. At least one of the partners is almost certain to be inflamed with sexual passion, Tolkien advised. This is especially true among the young, though Tolkien believed that such friendships might be possible later in life, "when sex cools down."

As any reader of Tolkien's works understands, Tolkien was a romantic at heart. He celebrated the fact that "in our Western culture the romantic chivalric tradition [is] still strong," though he recognized that "the times are inimical to it." Even so, as a concerned father, Tolkien warned Michael to avoid allowing his romantic instinct to lead him astray, fooled by "the flattery of sympathy nicely seasoned with a titillation of sex."

Beyond this, Tolkien demonstrated a profound understanding of male sexuality and the need for boundaries and restraint. Even as he was often criticized for having an overly negative understanding of male sexuality, Tolkien presented an honest assessment of the sex drive in a fallen world. He argued that men are not naturally monogamous. "Monogamy (although it has long been fundamental to our inherited ideas) is for us men a piece of 'revealed' ethic, according to faith and not to the flesh." In his own times, Tolkien had seen the binding power of cultural custom and moral tradition recede into the historical memory. With the sexual revolution already visible on the horizon, Tolkien believed that Christianity's revealed sex ethic would be the only force adequate to restrain the unbridled sexuality of fallen man. "Each of us could healthfully beget, in our 30 odd years of full manhood, a few hundred children, and enjoy the process," Tolkien admonished his son. Nevertheless, the joys and satisfactions of monogamous marriage provide the only true context for sexuality without shame. Furthermore, Tolkien was confident that Christianity's understanding of sex and marriage pointed to eternal as well as temporal pleasures.

Even as he celebrated the integrity of Christian marriage, Tolkien advised Michael that true faithfulness in marriage would require a continual exercise of the will. Even in marriage, there remains a demand for denial, he insisted. "Faithfulness in Christian marriage entails that: great mortification. For a Christian man there is no escape. Marriage may help to sanctify and direct to its proper object his sexual desires; its grace may help him in the struggle; but the struggle remains. It will not satisfy him—as hunger may be kept off by regular meals. It will offer as many difficulties to the purity proper to that state, as it provides easements. No man, however truly he loved his betrothed and bride as a young man, has lived faithful to her as a wife in mind and body without deliberate conscious exercise of the will, without self-denial."

Tolkien traced unhappiness in marriage, especially on the part of the husband, to the church's failure to teach these truths and to speak of marriage honestly. Those who see marriage as nothing more than the arena of ecstatic and romantic love will be disappointed, Tolkien understood. "When the glamour wears off, or merely works a bit thin, they think they have made a mistake, and that the real soul-mate is still to find. The real soul-mate too often proves to be the next sexually attractive person that comes along."

With these words, Tolkien advised his middle son that marriage is an objective reality that is honorable in the eyes of God. Thus, marriage defines its own satisfactions. The integrity of Christian marriage requires a man to exercise his will even in the arena of love and to commit all of his sexual energy and passion to the honorable estate of marriage, refusing himself even the imagination of violating his marital vows.

In a letter to his friend C. S. Lewis, Tolkien advised, "Christian marriage is not a prohibition of sexual intercourse, but the correct way of sexual temperance—in fact probably the best way of getting the most satisfying sexual pleasure." In the face of a world increasingly committed to sexual anarchy, Tolkien understood that sex must be respected as a volatile and complex gift, bearing potential for great pleasure and even greater pain.

With deep moral insight, Tolkien understood that those who give themselves most unreservedly to sexual pleasure will derive the least pleasure and fulfillment in the end. As author Joseph Pearce, one of Tolkien's most insightful interpreters explains, sexual temperance is necessary "because man does not live on sex alone." Temperance and restraint represent "the moderate path between prudishness and prurience, the two extremes of sexual obsession," Pearce expands.

Explicit references to sexuality are virtually missing from Tolkien's published works, allegories, fables, and stories. Nevertheless, sex is always in the background as part of the moral landscape. Joseph Pearce understands this clearly, arguing that Tolkien's literary characters "are certainly not sexless in the sense of being asexual but, on the contrary, are archetypically and stereotypically sexual." Pearce makes this claim notwithstanding the fact that there is no sexual activity or overt sexual enticement found in Tolkien's tales.

How is this possible? In a profound employment of the moral spirit, Tolkien presented his characters in terms of honor and virtue, with heroic men demonstrating classical masculine virtues and the heroines appearing as women of honor, valor, and purity.

Nevertheless, we would be hard pressed to appreciate Tolkien's understanding of sex, marriage, and family if we did not have considerable access into the realities of Tolkien's family and his role as both husband and father. Tolkien's letters, especially those written to his three sons, show the loving concern of a devoted father, as well as the rare literary gift Tolkien both possessed and employed with such power. The letter Tolkien wrote Michael in the year 1941—with the world exploding in war and civilization coming apart at its seams—is a model of fatherly concern, counsel, and instruction.

From the vantage point of the twenty-first century,

Tolkien will appear to many to be both out of step and out of tune with the sexual mores of our times. Tolkien would no doubt take this as a sincere, if unintended, compliment. He knew he was out of step, and he steadfastly refused to update his morality in order to pass the muster of the moderns. Writing to Christopher, his youngest son, Tolkien explained this well: "We were born in a dark age out of due time (for us). But there is this comfort: otherwise we should not know, or so much love, what we do love. I imagine the fish out of water is the only fish to have an inkling of water." Thanks to these letters, we have more than an inkling of what Tolkien meant.

2

A NEW LOOK AT LUST

A Secular View

When philosopher Simon Blackburn was invited to present a lecture on one of the seven deadly sins, he feared he would be asked to address sloth. "I did worry," he said, "not because of unfamiliarity with the vice, but because of doubts about having the energy to find something to say about it."

As it turned out, Blackburn was not invited to speak about sloth. Instead, he was invited to address the issue of lust, and on that topic he found enough energy to say a good deal about a vice that has driven humanity throughout the ages. Lust, Blackburn argues, "gets a bad press." His objective, based on his lecture sponsored by the New York Public Library and Oxford

University Press, is to rescue lust from misunderstandings and historical abuse. He does acknowledge that lust has a bad reputation: "It's the fly in the ointment, the black sheep of the family, the ill-bred, trashy cousin of upstanding members like love and friendship. It lives on the wrong side of the tracks, lumbers around elbowing its way into too much of our lives, and blushes when it comes into company."

Blackburn is a philosopher of wide reputation who has taught at the University of North Carolina, Oxford University, and the University of Cambridge. He is an excellent writer who combines both style and wit. In recent years, he has written *Think* and *Being Good,* two works intended to introduce philosophical subjects to a general readership. In those books, Blackburn presents a fundamentally secular understanding of life and a rather dispassionate engagement with philosophical and moral issues.

In his new book, *Lust,* Blackburn presents an updated vision of lust as sexual desire for its own sake.[1] If lust now has a bad press, Blackburn wants to be its public relations agent. Lust is inevitably compared

---

1. Simon Blackburn, *Lust: The Seven Deadly Sins* (New York: Oxford University Press, 2006).

with love. Blackburn understands the quandary, noting, "We smile at lovers holding hands in the park. But we wrinkle our noses if we find them acting out their lust under the bushes. Love receives the world's applause. Lust is furtive, ashamed, and embarrassed. Love pursues the good of the other, with self-control, concern, reason, and patience. Lust pursues its own gratification, headlong, impatient of any control, immune to reason." As a moral philosopher, Blackburn understands that love requires knowledge, reason, and time, combined with truth and trust. Lust, on the other hand, is symbolized by "a trail of clothing in the hallway" that represents a loss of reason, self-control, and discipline.

Needless to say, lust has been a part of human desire and human experience ever since the Fall. Blackburn, who provides no evidence of even believing in anything like sin, sees lust as one of the greatest moral challenges facing modern individuals. "Living with lust," he says, "is like living shackled to a lunatic." Frankly, it's hard to improve upon that description.

Much of the difficulty in addressing the issue of lust in our modern times can be traced to the highly sexualized character of contemporary culture. Even if lust is reducible to sexual desire (rather than desire for

power, money, or other goods), it is increasingly difficult to separate lust from the ordering of everyday life.
Sex has lost its public shamefulness; moral boundaries
have been pulled down in the name of moral
"progress"; and overt sexuality now drives much of our
entertainment, advertising, and cultural conversation.
How is lust to be separated from all that?

Blackburn defines lust as "the enthusiastic desire,
the desire that infuses the body, for sexual activity and
its pleasures for their own sake." That definition is
more sophisticated than it may at first appear. Blackburn combines powerful concepts like enthusiasm, desire, sexual activity, and pleasure, but he focuses his definition of lust on the desire for sexual pleasure for its
own sake. This elevation of sexual desire, stripped of
moral context and boundaries, well represents lust as it
appears in our contemporary world.

The ancients identified the seven deadly sins as
pride, greed, lust, envy, gluttony, anger, and sloth. The
entire panoply of human sinfulness was, they believed,
traced to one of these root sins and the deadly effects
that follow. The Christian church embraced the notion
of the seven deadly sins and joined them to the seven
heavenly virtues, identified as prudence, temperance,
justice, fortitude, faith, hope, and charity. Presumably,

temperance was designed to limit lust, but lust appears to have gained the upper hand.

Tracing the idea of lust through Western thought, Blackburn rejects the common association of lust with excess. Lust is not really about excessive desire, argues Blackburn, but rather a desire for sexual pleasure as an end in itself. Lust met disaster in the form of the Stoics, who feared a life ruled by passion rather than reason. The Roman philosopher Seneca popularized a Stoic philosophy in adopting as his motto "Nothing for pleasure's sake." Seneca argued that lust was to be overcome for the survival of humanity, even as sexuality was to be directed only toward "the continuation of the human race." Of course, Seneca made this argument about lust in a letter he wrote to his mother, so it is difficult to know how seriously to take his description. Nevertheless, Blackburn takes him at his word.

But if the Stoics represented a significant setback for lust, this deadly sin met its deadliest opponent in Christianity. Blackburn describes this as "the Christian panic" that directed moral scrutiny to sexual pleasure itself, not just to what might be considered excess. Predictably, Blackburn directs his attention to Augustine, the fourth-century bishop whose views on sex have influenced at least fifteen centuries of Christian thought.

Augustine, whose youth had been given to sexual excess, was determined after his conversion to deny that sexual pleasure was a part of the Creator's design for human sexuality, even from the beginning. Had the Fall not occurred, Augustine argued, sex would be a purely rational affair, untainted by any physical pleasure. Copulation would be, in effect, just like shaking hands. Later, as represented in the thoughts of Thomas Aquinas, the church argued that sexuality was defined both by scriptural command and the revelation found in nature. This additional dimension of lust was directed at the unnatural desires evident in much of humanity.

Blackburn's purpose is to overcome all pessimism toward lust. He even defends the use of pornography, which can, he argues, point toward the higher purposes of sex, rather than the lower degradations. He takes on the evolutionary psychologists, arguing that their naturalistic view of sex is too mechanistic. But his main effort is to overcome what he sees as Christianity's pessimism toward sexual desire as an end in itself. In effect, Blackburn's effort is to deny that lust should be considered a sin at all, deadly or otherwise.

Blackburn's short book does not answer all the questions he raises. Even as he attacks Christian "pessimism" and calls for lust to be accepted as a universal human reality, Blackburn does not call for the removal of all moral boundaries on human sexuality. In the end, *Lust* is a fascinating little treatise offered by a prominent intellectual, safely removed from the hard moral decisions of everyday life. His view of lust is not only sanitized, it is more deeply rooted in literature than in life. Perhaps this is due to Blackburn's profession as an academic philosopher, or perhaps it is because a modern secular philosopher can talk about sex only in the context of irony.

The Christian worldview finds congruence with Blackburn on this essential point—that lust is best described as a desire for sexual pleasure as an end in itself. Augustine aside, there is no biblical reason to suspect that sex before the Fall would have been devoid of physical pleasure. Indeed, we have every reason to believe that sexual pleasure is one of God's sweetest gifts to His human creatures. Sexual desire—and the promise of sexual pleasure—is meant to draw us into marriage, toward children, and into fidelity and responsibility. Lust is sinful precisely to the extent that sexual desire and passion are stripped from this moral context. In a God-centered worldview, nothing on earth can be seen as an end in itself. Nothing is to be understood as existing for its own sake.

Sexual desire for its own sake is sexual desire stripped of the Creator's glory and stolen from its moral context. What Blackburn celebrates, Christianity rightly condemns. Intentionally or not, Simon Blackburn has put lust back on the line for debate, and his lecture-turned-essay is about as thoughtful a secular defense of lust as we are likely to find. There is, of course, an altogether different understanding of lust, but it is not to be expected from a secular worldview. Christianity alone can explain why lust—and sin in every form—is so deadly.

3

ANOTHER LOOK AT LUST

The Christian View

I f Simon Blackburn takes lust to be an object of celebration, Joshua Harris understands that it is a danger to be taken with the utmost seriousness. In *Not Even a Hint: Guarding Your Heart Against Lust,* Harris provides a candid appraisal of lust as a challenge for the Christian believer.[1] According to Harris, lust is wrongly directed desire. "To lust is to want what you don't have and weren't meant to have," he explains.

---

1. Joshua Harris, *Not Even a Hint: Guarding Your Heart Against Lust* (Sisters, OR: Multnomah, 2003). Used by permission.

"Lust goes beyond attraction, and appreciation of beauty, or even a healthy desire for sex—it makes these desires more important than God. Lust wants to go outside God's guidelines to find satisfaction."

Harris's approach is countercultural from the start. Most Americans reject the very notion that there are any pleasures that we are not meant to have. Our society has institutionalized lust, weaving the patterns of illicit sexual desire throughout the culture's interplay of media, entertainment, status, and advertising. Lust is now part and parcel of the modern vision of the good life. Harris argues that "lust may be the defining struggle for this generation." Previous generations faced the moral challenges of war, poverty, and pestilence, but this generation is absorbed in a continual cycle of lust and sexual gratification.

A best-selling author, Harris is known to many young Christians through his works on biblical courtship and marriage. In *I Kissed Dating Goodbye* and *Boy Meets Girl,* he helped to educate a generation of evangelicals about the biblical notion of courtship as preparation for marriage. Senior pastor of Covenant Life Church in Gaithersburg, Maryland, Harris combines pastoral experience with keen spiritual insight. In his earlier works, he focused on the dangers inherent in the conventional pattern of dating that has become the norm among young Americans. This system of one-on-one dating between young men and women is morally suspect because it places the couple in a context of premature sexual intimacy. The escalating rate of premarital sex among young Americans—including many who claim to be Christians—is sufficient evidence to give Harris's arguments credence. Furthermore, he roots his argument in a more biblical vision of courtship as intentional preparation for marriage.

Why choose now to write on lust? "Writing two books on the topic of dating and courtship in the last five years has helped me to see just how serious this problem is for a broad spectrum of believers," Harris explains. "I've received thousands of letters and e-mails from people of all ages around the world who are struggling with sexual impurity." As Harris sees it, the problem is deadly serious. "The stories are heartbreaking, and they're from both women and men. They're stories of small compromises that lead to serious sin and regret. They're stories of secret and anguishing battles with premarital sex, with pornography, and with homosexuality. They're stories from those who once swore to remain pure and now can't believe the depths of impurity to which they've descended." With lust now standing at the center of American culture and even celebrated as a vital part of the "good life," Harris sounds like an absolute extremist when it comes to the seriousness of lust. What is God's standard when it comes to lust? How much lust is allowable in the Christian life? Harris's answer is the essence of simplicity: "Nada. Zip. Zero." Just in case you missed his point, Harris goes on to insist that lust has no place at all in the Christian life—not even a hint.

Why such a high standard? "I'm not saying this to be dramatic," Harris insists. "I really believe it's what God calls each Christian to regardless of what kind of culture we live in or how old we are. And it's not because God is heavy-handed, or strict for the sake of strictness. It's because He loves us—and because we are His." Joshua Harris is an honest man, and he brings that honesty to *Not Even a Hint.* He confesses his own struggle with lust as a young man and allows readers— both male and female—to identify with the depth of his moral and spiritual struggle.

When addressing lust, defined as an illicit sexual desire, the chief difficulty we face is in defining the distinction between lust and a healthy sexual desire. Harris admits the difficulty, and he attempts to draw the distinction by insisting that lust is not being attracted to someone, nor is it a sudden eruption of sexual temptation. The essence of lust is the enjoyment of the illicit desire, the pleasure of temptation prolonged. Nevertheless, even innocent desire can turn into lust if given the slightest invitation. As Harris explains, "A sexual thought that pops into your mind isn't necessarily lust, but it can quickly become lust if it's entertained and dwelled on. An excitement for sex in marriage isn't sin, but it can be tainted by lust if it's not tempered with patience and restraint."

The human sex drive is not the product of biological evolution or cosmic accident. Our Creator made us sexual beings and put a strong sex drive within us in order to drive us toward marriage and all the goods that are united in the marital union. As fallen creatures, we need the guiding assistance of the sex drive to pull us out of lethargy and self-centeredness into a fruitful and faithful relationship with a spouse. In making us male and female, God intended for men to be sexually attracted to women and for women to be sexually attracted to men. This attraction is not merely a matter of mutuality between two genders but is intended to direct us toward a mutuality of two persons, united in the covenant of marriage. Within marriage, sexual pleasure and sexual passion are essential parts of the relational glue that holds the union together, points toward pro-creation, and establishes an intimacy described in the Bible as a one-flesh relationship. Joshua Harris under-stands this, and he affirms that "God gave us our drives so that we would drive toward something."

The deadly problem of lust arises when the sex drive is directed toward something less than or other than the purity of marriage. This Christian under-standing of lust could not be more different from the secular argument of Simon Blackburn. Where Black-burn defines sexual passion and pleasure as ends in themselves, leading to an open embrace of lust as an act of self-definition, Harris's Christian worldview leads him to see lust as a reminder of the believer's need for self-denial. He understands the fact that we live in a pornographic age and in a society driven by lust. Given these realities, he proposes a "custom-tailored plan" for every individual. With the complex and immediately available seductions of pornography and sexual entice-ment, Harris understands that every individual is likely to be faced with a different pattern of temptation. As he acknowledges, "There can be no 'one size fits all' approach to combating lust." That being the case, the Christian is required to be honest about the pattern of temptation he or she faces. Whether it comes packaged and presented in books, on the Internet, in the mailbox, or in the general context of everyday life, Harris points to the need for accountability and ruthless honesty about lust and its consequences.

Having been there himself, Harris also knows that the struggle against lust cannot be won by mere personal determination and the application of self-control. Furthermore, legalism is no antidote to lust. "We can't save ourselves and we can't change ourselves," he explains. "Only faith in Christ can rescue us from the prison of our sin. And only the Spirit can transform us. Our job is to invite His work, participate with it, and submit more and more of our thoughts, actions, and desires to Him."

Simon Blackburn thinks that lust is a virtue, and many Christians fool themselves into thinking that lust is no real problem. Joshua Harris has offered an antidote to those tragic misperceptions. Lust is not only a vice; it is a sin that ignites yet other sins.

4

PORNOGRAPHY AND THE INTEGRITY OF CHRISTIAN MARRIAGE

The Challenge

The intersection of pornography and marriage is one of the most problematic issues among many couples today, including Christian couples. The pervasive plague of pornography represents one of the greatest moral challenges faced by the Christian church in the postmodern age. With eroticism woven into the very heart of the culture, celebrated in its entertainment, and advertised as a commodity, it is virtually impossible to escape the pervasive influence of pornography in our culture and in our lives. At the same time, the problem of human sinfulness is fundamentally unchanged from the time of the Fall until the present. There is no theological basis for assuming that human beings are more lustful, more defenseless in the face of sexual temptation, or more susceptible to the corruption of sexual desire than was the case in any previous generation.

Two distinctions mark the present age from previous eras. First, pornography has been so mainstreamed through advertising, commercial images, entertainment, and everyday life that what would have been illegal just a few decades ago is now taken as common dress, common entertainment, and unremarkable sensuality. Second, explicit eroticism—complete with pornographic images, narrative, and symbolism—is now celebrated as a cultural good in some sectors of the society. Pornography, now reported to be the seventh-largest business in America, claims its own icons and public figures. Hugh Hefner, founder of *Playboy,* is considered by many Americans to be a model of entrepreneurial success, sexual pleasure, and a liberated lifestyle. The use of Hugh Hefner as a spokesman by a family-based hamburger chain in California indicates something of how pornography has been mainstreamed in the culture.

Growing out of those two developments is a third reality—namely, that increased exposure to erotic stimulation creates the need for ever-increasing stimulation in order to demand notice, arouse sexual interest, and retain attention. In an odd twist, hyperexposure to pornography leads to a lower net return on investment, which is to say that the more pornography one sees, the more explicit the images must be in order to excite interest. Thus, in order to sustain the excitement of "transgressing," as the postmodernist would put it, pornographers must continue to push the envelope.

One further qualification must be added to this picture. Pornography is mainly, though not exclusively, a *male* phenomenon. That is to say, the users and consumers of pornography are overwhelmingly male—boys and men. In the name of women's liberation, some pornography directed toward a female market has emerged in recent years. Nevertheless, this is decidedly a niche market in the larger pornographic economy. The fact remains that many men pay a great deal of money and spend a great deal of time looking *at* and looking *for* pornographic images in order to arouse themselves sexually.

Why is pornography such a big business? The answer to that question lies in two basic realities. First, the most fundamental answer to the question must be rooted in a biblical understanding of human beings as sinners. We must take into full account the fact that sin has corrupted every good thing in creation, and the effects of sin extend to every dimension of life. The sex drive, which should point toward covenant fidelity in marriage and all the goods associated with that most basic institution, has instead been corrupted to devastating effect. Rather than being directed toward fidelity, covenantal commitment, procreation, and the wonder of a one-flesh relationship, the sex drive has been degraded into a passion that robs God of His glory, celebrates the sensual at the expense of the spiritual, and sets what God had intended for good on a path that leads to destruction in the name of personal fulfillment. The most important answer we can give to pornography's rise in popularity is rooted in the Christian doctrine of sin. As sinners, we corrupt what God has perfectly designed for the good of His creatures, and we have turned sex into a carnival of orgiastic pleasures. Not only have we severed sex from marriage, but as a society, we now look at marriage as an imposition, chastity as an embarrassment, and sexual restraint as a psychological hang-up. The doctrine of sin explains why we have exchanged the glory of God for Sigmund Freud's concept of "polymorphous perversity."

In addition to this, we must recognize that a capitalist free-market economy rewards those who produce a product that is both attractive and appetitive. The purveyors of pornography know that they succeed by directing their product to the lowest common denominator of humanity—a depraved sexual mind. Without the legal restraints common in previous generations, pornographers are now free to sell their goods virtually without restriction. Beyond this, they base their marketing plans on the assumption that an individual can be seduced into the use of pornography and will then be hooked into a pattern of dependence upon pornographic images and the need for increasingly explicit sexual material as a means of sexual arousal.

The bottom line is that, in our sinfulness, men are drawn toward pornography, and a frighteningly large percentage of men develop a dependence upon pornographic images for their own sexual arousal and for their concept of the good life, sexual fulfillment, and even meaning in life. Medical research has documented the increased flow of endorphins, hormones that create pleasure in the brain, when sexual images are viewed. Given the law of reduced effect, greater stimulation is needed to keep a constant flow of endorphins to the brain's pleasure centers. Without conscious awareness of what is happening, men are drawn into a pattern of deeper and deeper sin, more and more explicit pornography, and never-ending rationalization. And it all started when the eye first began its perusal of the pornographic image and sexual arousal was its product.

The postmodern age has brought many wonders as well as incredible moral challenges. Often, technological achievement and moral complexity come hand in hand. This is most explicitly the case with the development of the Internet. For the first time in human history, a teenager in his bedroom has access to an innumerable array of pornographic Web sites, catering to every imaginable sexual passion, perversion, and pleasure. Today's teenager, if not stranded on some desert island, is likely to know more about sex and its complexities than his father knew when he got married. Furthermore, what most generations have known only in the imagination—if at all—is now there for the viewing on Web sites, both commercial and free. The Internet has brought an interstate highway of pornography into every community, with entrance ramps at every home computer.

Pornography represents one of the most insidious attacks upon the sanctity of marriage and the goodness of sex within the one-flesh relationship. The celebration of debauchery rather than purity, the elevation of genital pleasure over all other considerations, and the corruption of sexual energy through an inversion of the self—all this corrupts the idea of marriage, leads to incalculable harm, and subverts both marriage and the marital bond.

5

PORNOGRAPHY AND THE INTEGRITY OF CHRISTIAN MARRIAGE

The Calling

The Christian worldview must direct all consideration of sexuality to the institution of marriage. Marriage is not merely the arena for sexual activity; it is presented in Scripture as the divinely designed arena for the display of God's glory on earth as a man and a woman come together in a one-flesh relationship within the marriage covenant. Rightly understood and rightly ordered, marriage is a picture of God's own covenantal faithfulness. Marriage is to display God's

glory, reveal God's good gifts to His creatures, and protect human beings from the inevitable disaster that fol-
lows when sexual passions are divorced from their
rightful place.

The marginalization of marriage, and the open
antipathy with which many of the cultural elite approach the question of marriage, produces a context in
which Christians committed to a marriage ethic appear
hopelessly out of step with the larger culture. Whereas
the larger society sees marriage as a privatized contract
to be made and unmade at will, Christians must see
marriage as an inviolable covenant made before God
and man that establishes both temporal and eternal
realities.

Christians have no right to be embarrassed when it
comes to talking about sex and sexuality. An unhealthy
reticence or embarrassment in dealing with these issues
is a form of disrespect to God's creation. Whatever
God made is good, and every good thing God made
has an intended purpose that ultimately reveals His
own glory. When conservative Christians respond to
sexual matters with ambivalence or embarrassment, we
slander the goodness of God and hide His glory, which
is intended to be revealed in the right use of creation's
gifts.

Therefore, our first responsibility is to point all persons toward the right use of God's good gifts and the legitimacy of sex in marriage as vital aspects of God's intention in marriage from the beginning. Many individuals—especially young men—hold a false expectation of what sex represents within the marriage relationship. Since the male sex drive is largely directed toward genital pleasure, men often assume that women are just the same. While physical pleasure is certainly an essential part of the female experience of sex, a woman is not as focused on the solitary goal of genital fulfillment as is the case with many men. A biblical worldview understands that God has demonstrated His glory in both the similarities and the differences that mark men and women. Alike made in the image of God, men and women are literally made *for* each other. The physicality of the male and female bodies cries out for fulfillment in the other. The sex drive calls both men and women out of themselves and toward a covenantal relationship that is consummated in a one-flesh union. By definition, sex within marriage is not merely the accomplishment of sexual fulfillment on the part of two individuals who happen to share the same bed. Rather, it is mutual self-giving that reaches pleasures both physical and spiritual. The emotional aspect of sex cannot be divorced from its physical dimension. Though men are often tempted to forget this, women possess more- and less-gentle means of making that need clear.

Consider the fact that a woman has every right to expect that her husband will earn access to the marriage bed. As the apostle Paul states, the husband and wife no longer own their own bodies, but each now belongs to the other (see 1 Corinthians 7:4). At the same time, Paul instructed men to love their wives even as Christ has loved the church (see Ephesians 5:25). Even as wives are commanded to submit to the authority of their husbands (see verse 22), the husband is called to a far higher standard of Christlike love and devotion toward his wife. Therefore, when I say that a husband must regularly "earn" privileged access to the marital bed, I mean that a husband owes his wife the confidence, affection, and emotional support that would lead her to freely give herself to her husband in the act of sex.

God's gift of sexuality is inherently designed to pull us out of ourselves and toward our spouse. For men, this means that marriage calls us out of our self-focused concern for genital pleasure and toward the totality of the sex act within the marital relationship. Put most bluntly, I believe that God means for a man to be civilized by, and directed and stimulated toward, marital faithfulness by the fact that his wife will freely give herself to him sexually only when he presents himself as worthy of her attention and desire.

Perhaps specificity will help to illustrate this point. I am confident that God's glory is seen in the fact that a married man, faithful to his wife, who loves her genuinely, will wake up in the morning driven by ambition and passion in order to make his wife proud, confident, and assured in her devotion to him. A husband who looks forward to sex with his wife will aim his life toward those things that will bring rightful pride to her heart, will direct himself to her with love as the foundation of their relationship, and will present himself to her as a man in whom she can take both pride and satisfaction.

Consider these two pictures. The first picture is of a man who has set himself toward a commitment to sexual purity and is living in sexual integrity with his wife. In order to fulfill his wife's rightful expectations and to maximize their mutual pleasure in the marriage bed, he is careful to live, talk, lead, and love in such a way that his wife finds her fulfillment in giving herself to him in love. The sex act then becomes a fulfillment of their entire relationship, not an isolated physical act that is merely incidental to their love for each other. Neither uses sex as a means of manipulation, neither is inordinately focused merely on self-centered personal pleasure, and both give themselves to each other in un-apologetic and unhindered sexual passion. In this pic-ture, there is no shame. Before God, this man can be confident that he is fulfilling his responsibilities both as a *male* and as a *man*. He is directing his sexuality, his sex drive, and his physical embodiment toward the one-flesh relationship that is the perfect paradigm of God's intention in creation.

By contrast, consider another man. This man lives alone, or at least in a context other than holy marriage. Directed inwardly rather than outwardly, his sex drive has become an engine for lust and self-gratification. Pornography is the essence of his sexual interest and arousal. Rather than taking satisfaction in a wife, he looks at dirty pictures in order to be rewarded with sex-ual arousal that comes without responsibility, expecta-tion, or demand. Arrayed before him are a seemingly endless variety of naked women, sexual images of ex-plicit carnality, and a cornucopia of perversions in-tended to seduce the imagination and corrupt the soul. This man need not be concerned with his physical appearance, his personal hygiene, or his moral character in the eyes of a wife. Without this structure and accountability, he is free to take his sexual pleasure without regard for his unshaved face, his slothfulness, his halitosis, his body odor, or his physical appearance. He faces no requirement of personal respect, and no eyes gaze upon him in order to evaluate the seriousness and worthiness of his sexual desire. Instead, his eyes roam across the images of unblinking faces, leering at women who make no demands upon him, who never speak back, and who can never say no. There is no exchange of respect, no exchange of love, and nothing more than the using of women as sex objects for his individual and inverted sexual pleasure.

These two pictures of male sexuality are deliberately intended to drive home the point that every man must decide who he will be, whom he will serve, and how he will love. In the end, a man's decision about pornography is a decision about his soul, a decision about his marriage, a decision about his wife, and a decision about his God.

Pornography is a slander against the goodness of God's creation and a corruption of this good gift God has given His creatures out of His own self-giving love. To abuse this gift is to weaken not only the institution of marriage but the fabric of civilization itself. To choose lust over love is to debase humanity and to worship the false god Priapus in the most brazen form of modern idolatry.

The deliberate use of pornography is nothing less than the willful invitation of illicit lovers, objectified sex objects, and forbidden knowledge into a man's heart, mind, and soul. The damage to the man's heart is beyond measure, and the cost in human misery will only be made clear on the Day of Judgment. From the moment each boy reaches puberty until the day he is lowered into the ground, every man will struggle with lust. Let us follow the biblical example and scriptural command that we make a covenant with our eyes lest we sin. In this society, we are called to be nothing less than a corps of the mutually accountable amidst a world that lives as if it will never be called to account.

6

HOMOSEXUALITY IN THEOLOGICAL PERSPECTIVE

The Roots of a Movement

In every age the church is confronted with cultural and ethical challenges that test both the conviction and the compassion of the body of Christ. Since World War II, American Christians have struggled with issues of racism, war, abortion, and sexuality in successive and overlapping waves of moral confrontation. In the end, the issues of abortion and homosexuality are likely to prove the two most divisive issues Americans have faced since the Civil War.

The issue of homosexuality is currently the most heated front in the so-called culture war. Homosexual activist groups are pressing for identification of homosexual men and lesbians as a class offered special protections under civil rights legislation, and homosexual-oriented literature is now commonplace in public libraries—and even in some public schools. The wider secular academy has largely capitulated to the homosexual movement, and gay studies programs are now a growth industry in the academic culture. Moreover, the mainstream media now portray homosexuality in a positive light. Openly homosexual characters on prime-time television are joined by overt homoerotic images in broad-based advertising. More distressing, most of the historic denominations of the older Protestant mainline are debating homosexuality, with the issue currently focused on the ordination of practicing homosexuals to the ministry.

How did this happen? The origins of the homosexual movement as a major cultural force must be traced to the 1969 Stonewall riots in Manhattan. Known within the homosexual community as the Stonewall Rebellion, the riot took place as New York City police raided a homosexual bar. The patrons fought back in what would become the inaugural symbol of the gay liberation movement. As the *Village Voice* reported on July 3, 1969, " 'Gay power' erected its brazen head and spat out a fairy tale the likes of which the area has never seen…. Watch out. The liberation is underway."

What has followed has been a measured and strategic effort to win the legitimization of homosexuality, to promote homosexual themes in the media, and to secure for homosexuals special entitlements as a legally protected class. Furthermore, the movement has pushed for specific policy goals, such as the removal of all antisodomy laws, the recognition of homosexual partnerships on par with heterosexual marriage, the enactment of antidiscrimination laws, and the removal of all barriers to homosexuals in the military, the academy, business, and churches.

In order to pursue these goals, the homosexual movement has organized itself as a liberation movement, based on an ideology of liberation from oppression that finds its roots in Marxist philosophies. Thus, the intention has been to identify with other liberation movements, including the civil rights movement and the feminist agenda. But the goal is not merely the legitimization of homosexual activity or even the recognition of homosexual relationships. Rather, it is the creation of a public homosexual culture within the American mainstream.

This movement is a stark challenge to all sectors of American society. It has become the driving engine of a social revolution that will influence or transform every institution of American life, from the family to mediating institutions to the state. Even beyond this, an evangelical perspective must recognize that such a revolution is an attack upon the foundations of gender, family, sexuality, and morality—all of which are central issues of the Christian worldview based on the Word of God revealed in holy Scripture. Thus, this is a challenge evangelicals must not fail to meet with both grace and honesty.

The homosexual movement did not spring from a vacuum. Indeed, the challenge has emerged from within the context of the seismic culture shift which has transformed Western societies during the twentieth century. The concept of a culture shift draws attention to the pattern of fundamental changes that have shaped every level of social and cultural life. A culture shift is nothing less than a fundamental reordering of society in terms of structures, ideologies, worldviews, morality, and patterns of knowledge.

The culture shift from modernity to postmodernity has affected all "communities of meaning," to use the category favored by sociologists. From the Christian perspective, the most important category is truth, and the culture shift has radically reordered how Americans view the issue of truth. The last half of the twentieth century has proven that the left wing of the Enlightenment has finally won the day. Whereas most pre-Enlightenment persons understood truth to be an objective reality to which they must submit when it is made known, modern Americans view truth as a private commodity to be shaped, accepted, or rejected according to one's own personal preference or taste. Indeed, a majority of American adults now reject the very notion of absolute truth.

All matters of faith and morality are now considered by a majority of Americans to be issues of mere private preference. All truth is interior and privatized. This embrace of undiluted individualism underlies our current cultural confusion. The successive and progressive shift in the locus of truth and authority from the Christian worldview to the state to the isolated individual leaves the American public unarmed for authentic moral discourse. All that remains is utter subjectivity and the inevitable power struggles which will occur when ideologies and political agendas clash in the public square.

Clearly, many who consider themselves believing

Christians have succumbed to the lure of relativistic worldviews. Yet Christians must face squarely the truth that the faith once for all delivered to the saints is fundamentally incompatible with a rejection of absolute truth. The gospel itself is a direct claim to universal and absolute truth, and the Bible (which is incomprehensible apart from its claim to absolute truth as revealed by God Himself) makes a claim to truth that applies to all persons everywhere and in all times. If there is no absolute truth, there is no Christian faith and there is no salvation through Jesus Christ, who made an absolute and universal claim when He declared Himself "the way, and the truth, and the life" (John 14:6).

Hence we see the culture war that now marks the life of the American republic. The issues of sexuality and abortion—and the entire controversy of political correctness—are but fronts and battle lines within the culture war. Christians must be armed for this conflict, and this will be possible only by means of a recovery of biblical faith and convictional courage.

One of the most formative shifts in the nation's public consciousness is the reduction of moral argumentation to what Harvard Law School professor Mary Ann Glendon terms "rights talk." All moral debates, whether about divorce, sex, abortion, or smoking tobacco, are now reduced to debates over individual rights, couched in the language of a "right to choose," a "right to sexual preference," or a "right to integrity or personhood," however determined. Our collective moral imagination has shifted from matters of right and wrong to mere contests for your rights, my rights, and their rights.

Here we see the corrosive effects of the acids of modernity. One of the most important aspects of this corrosion is the process of secularization, which has pervasively denuded the public square of all Christian truth claims, including and especially those related to moral truths. Beyond the public square, however, we must admit the impact of secularization within the church as well. Secularization is not something that has merely "happened" to the church. In very real ways, the church has aided and abetted that process by denying biblical truth and its claims to all dimensions of life.

The rise and tactical success of the homosexual movement was only made possible by the radical decline of the Christian worldview within Western culture. The Christian gospel makes a comprehensive claim to all areas of life and thought. Biblical truth is to be applied to all areas of life and all issues of individual and communal meaning. But moral relativism and rights talk have filled the vacuum left by the evacuation of the Christian worldview.

7

HOMOSEXUALITY IN THEOLOGICAL PERSPECTIVE

The Hermeneutic of Legitimization

The issue of homosexuality is a "first-order" theological issue as it presents itself in the current cultural debate. Fundamental truths essential to the Christian faith are at stake in this confrontation. These truths range from the most basic issues of theism to biblical authority; the nature of human beings; God's purpose and prerogatives in creation; sin, salvation, and sanctification; and, by extension, the entire body of evangelical divinity. Put bluntly, if the claims put forward by the homosexual movement are true, the entire system of the Christian faith is compromised, and some essential truths will fall.

Lest this be seen as an overstatement, consider the issue of biblical authority and inspiration. If the claims of revisionist exegetes are valid, then the very notions of verbal inspiration and biblical inerrancy are invalidated. But the challenge is yet deeper, for if, as the revisionist interpreters claim, holy Scripture can be so wrong and misdirected on this issue (to which it speaks so unambiguously), then the evangelical paradigm of biblical authority cannot stand.

As is the case with most ideological campaigns directed at the church, the homosexual movement comes complete with a well-defined hermeneutic. In fact, politico-ideological crusades that aspire for influence within churches must develop and articulate what I will term a *hermeneutic of legitimization,* designed to provide at least the appearance of biblical sanction. Thus, biblical interpretation becomes contested territory between rival worldviews.

The homosexual movement has employed a well-documented hermeneutic of suspicion toward biblical texts that address homosexuality. Their efforts have been to prove that the actions proscribed in biblical passages (notably Genesis 19; Leviticus 18:22; and Leviticus 20:13) do not refer to consensual homosexual acts but rather to homosexual rape and prostitution. When that effort is crushed on the shores of reality, they then suggest that, though the passages do in fact speak of homosexual acts, they reveal a patriarchal and oppressive bias that must be rejected by the contemporary church. Furthermore, it is commonly argued, Paul did not know of the reality of homosexual orientation, and thus Romans 1:26–27 must be read as if it referred to homosexual acts on the part of otherwise heterosexual persons.

The net result of this hermeneutic of legitimization has been confusion in the church. It has become the standard and politically correct perspective assumed in most sectors of the academy, and it is increasingly prevalent among members of the mainline Protestant denominations. Disappointingly, a number of evangelicals have been taken in as well.

An early attempt at revising the church's view of homosexuality was undertaken by D. Sherwin Bailey in *Homosexuality and the Western Christian Tradition*,[1]

---

1. Derrick Sherwin Bailey, *Homosexuality and the Western Christian Tradition* (London: Longmans, Green, 1955).

but the most influential work came twenty-five years later with the publication of *Christianity, Social Tolerance, and Homosexuality* by John Boswell, a professor of history at Yale University.[2] Similar proposals have come from figures such as John J. McNeill, a former Jesuit expelled from the order for his views on homosexuality. The most significant recent contribution to this debate is L. William Countryman's *Dirt, Sex, and Greed.*[3]

The revisionist hermeneutic, as applied to Romans 1:26–27, has been employed to argue that the text means something quite different from the church's traditional interpretation. By employing circumventions, circumlocutions, and contortions, the text's meaning is revised so as to negate its judgment upon homosexuality.

The critical issue used by the revisionists as a hermeneutical device is the concept of sexual orientation. The modern "discovery" of sexual orientation is used to deny the truth claim made clearly and in-

2. John Boswell, *Christianity, Social Tolerance, and Homosexuality: Gay People in Western Europe from the Beginning of the Christian Era to the Fourteenth Century* (Chicago: University of Chicago Press, 1980).

3. L. William Countryman, *Dirt, Sex, and Greed: Sexual Ethics in the New Testament and Their Implications for Today,* rev. ed. (Minneapolis: Fortress, 2007).

escapably within the biblical text. For example, in regard to the Romans text, Janet Fishburn of Drew University Theological School argues, "Yet, some biblical scholars point out that this passage can only refer to the homosexual acts of heterosexual persons. This is because the writers of the Bible did not distinguish between homosexual orientation and same-gender sexual acts. If this distinction is accepted, the condemnation of homosexuality in Romans does not apply to the sexual acts of homosexual persons."[4]

Similarly, New Testament professor Victor Paul Furnish argued that since Paul was unaware of the modern concept of homosexual orientation, his rejection of homosexuality must itself be rejected: "Not only the terms, but the concepts of 'homosexual' and 'homosexuality,' were unknown in Paul's day. These terms like 'heterosexual,' 'heterosexuality,' 'bisexual' and 'bisexuality,' presuppose an understanding of human sexuality that was possible only with the advent of modern psychology and sociological analysis. The ancient writers were operating without the vaguest idea of what we have learned to call 'sexual orientation.'"[5]

---

4. Janet Fishburn, *Confronting the Idolatry of Family: A New Vision for the Household of God* (Nashville: Abingdon, 1991).

5. Victor Paul Furnish, *The Moral Teachings of Paul: Selected Issues* (Nashville: Abingdon, 1985), 85.

Just how far some are willing to go in an effort to contort the biblical text is made clear by Countryman. Again, the issue is the construct of sexual orientation: "Homosexual orientation has been increasingly recognized in our time as a given of human sexuality. While most people feel some sexual attraction to members of both the same and the opposite sex and, in the majority of these, attraction to the opposite sex dominates, there is a sizeable minority for whom sexual attraction to persons of the same sex is a decisive shaping factor of their sexual lives.... To deny an entire class of human beings the right peaceably and without harming others to pursue the kind of sexuality that corresponds to their nature is a perversion of the gospel."

These statements indicate the general approach taken by revisionist scholarship and the ever-widening scope of the revisionist sweep. The hermeneutic of legitimization has been stunningly effective in forming a culture that accepts homosexual behavior and denies the binding authority of clear biblical injunctions. But this trend is not limited to mainline Protestantism and liberal Roman Catholicism. Some who claim evangelical identity also share the same revisionist methodology and conclusions. In an article published in the evangelical journal *TSF Bulletin,* Kathleen E. Corley and

Karen J. Torjesen argue, "It would appear then that in Paul issues of sexuality are theologically related to hierarchy, and therefore the issues of biblical feminism and lesbianism are irrefutably intertwined.… In the end, it would seem that if the church is going to deal with the issues of sexuality it is also going to have to deal with hierarchy. We need to grapple with the possibility that our conflicts over the appropriate use of human sexuality may rather be conflicts rooted in a need to legitimate a traditional social structure which assigns men and women specific and unequal positions. Could it be that the continued affirmation of the primacy of heterosexual marriage is possibly also the affirmation of the necessity for the sexes to remain in hierarchically structured relationships? Is the threat to marriage really a threat to hierarch? Is that what makes same-sex relationships so threatening, so frightening?"[6]

The arguments appeal to modern therapeutic constructs such as the hypothetical "sexual orientation" and use these to call into judgment the meaning of the biblical text. The essence of the complex revisionist arguments comes down to this: either the biblical texts

<hr />

6. Kathleen E. Corley and Karen J. Torjesen, "Sexuality, Hierarchy, and Evangelicalism," *Theological Students Fellowship Bulletin* (March–April 1987), 10:23–27.

do not proscribe homosexuality, but have been mis-construed by an oppressive heterosexist and patriarchal church to deny homosexuals their rights; or the biblical texts do proscribe homosexuality, but are oppressive, heterosexist, and patriarchal in themselves, and thus must be rejected or radically reinterpreted in order to remove the scandal of oppression.

What must be transparently clear by now is that these revisionist methodologies and hermeneutics of legitimization deny the truth status of holy Scripture. The passages are not merely reinterpreted in light of clear historical-grammatical exegesis; they are subverted and denied by implication and direct assault. Few revisionists are as direct in their assault as William M. Kent, a member of the United Methodist Committee to Study Homosexuality. Kent asserted that "the scriptural texts in the Old and New Testaments condemning homosexual practice are neither inspired by God nor otherwise of enduring Christian value. Considered in the light of the best biblical, theological, scientific, and social knowledge, the biblical condemnation of homosexual practice is better understood as representing time-and-place bound cultural prejudice."[7]

---

7. "Report of the Committee to Study Homosexuality to the General Council on Ministries of the United Methodist Church," August 24, 1991.

But Kent is not alone. From Union Theological Seminary, Robin Scroggs puts his position plainly: "Quite clearly…I cannot in conscience accept the view that makes biblical injunctions into necessarily eternal ethical truths, independent of the historical and cultural context."[8] Strikingly, Gary David Comstock, Protestant chaplain at Wesleyan University argues, "Not to recognize, critique, and condemn Paul's equation of godlessness with homosexuality is dangerous. To remain within our respective Christian traditions and not challenge those passages that degrade and destroy us is to contribute to our own oppression.… Those passages will be brought up and used against us again and again until Christians demand their removal from the biblical canon or, at the very least, formally discredit their authority to prescribe behavior."[9]

Evangelicals must lay bare the nature of this assault on the integrity and authority of the biblical text. Christianity stands or falls upon the validity and integrity of the revelation claim made by holy Scripture. This challenge must be met directly and publicly, and evangelicals must call the exegetical bluff put forward

8. Robin Scroggs, *The New Testament and Homosexuality* (Philadelphia: Fortress, 1983), 123.

9. Gary David Comstock, *Gay Theology Without Apology* (Cleveland: Pilgrim Press, 1993), 43.

by the revisionists. The foundational assault must be addressed. The confessing church must not be intimidated, coerced, or compromised by the revisionists.

As theologian Elizabeth Achtemeier asserted, "The clearest teaching of Scripture is that God intended sexual intercourse to be limited to the marriage relationship of one man and one woman."[10] A clear reminder of what is at stake comes, interestingly enough, from Robin Lane Fox, a secular historian: "As for homosexuality, Paul and the other apostles agreed with the accepted Jewish view that it was deadly sin which provoked God's wrath. It led to earthquakes and natural disasters, which were evident in the fate of Sodom. The absence of Gospel teaching on the topic did not amount to tacit approval. All orthodox Christians knew that homosexuals went to Hell until a modern minority tried to make them forget it."[11]

Of course, "all orthodox Christians" also knew that *all* unrepentant and unredeemed sinners go to hell, and unrepentant homosexuals were in a very large company. But only in modern times have revisionists

---

10. Mark O'Keefe, "Gays and the Bible," The Virginian-Pilot (Norfolk, VA), February 14, 1993.

11. Robin Lane Fox, *Pagans and Christians* (New York: Alfred A. Knopf, 1987), 352.

tried to suggest with seriousness that the Bible is unclear on the issue of homosexuality and that the church must forfeit its traditional—and exegetically inescapable— understanding of the relevant biblical texts. The "modern minority" identified by Fox has been, nonetheless, stunningly successful in confusing the church.

HOMOSEXUALITY IN THEOLOGICAL PERSPECTIVE

A Biblical Worldview

Few modern concepts have been as influential as the psychosocial construct of sexual orientation. The concept is now firmly rooted in the national consciousness, and many Americans consider the concept to be thoroughly based in credible scientific research. The concept of sexual orientation was an intentional and quite successful attempt to redefine the debate over homosexuality from same-gender sexual acts to homosexual identity—that is, from what homosexuals *do* to who homosexuals *are*.

Yet this concept is actually of quite recent vintage. In fact, even within the past decade, the more common concept employed by the homosexual movement was *sexual preference.* The reason for the shift is clear. The use of the term *preference* implied a voluntary choice. The clinical category of *orientation* was more useful in public arguments.

The very notion of homosexuals as a category of persons constituted by sexual identity is a recent invention. The biblical revisionists cited in the previous chapter were correct when they asserted that the apostle Paul knew nothing of the category of sexual orientation. That concept is rooted in late nineteenth-century efforts to apply psychological categories to sexual behavior. As Marjorie Rosenberg writes, "From antiquity until perhaps a century ago, choice was presumed to govern sexual behavior. But in the late 19th century, with burgeoning medical science as midwife, a new kind of creature was born—'the homosexual'—his entire identity based upon his sexual preference."[1]

The argument would now be that homosexuals exist as a special class or category—a "third sex" along-

---

1. Marjorie Rosenberg, "Inventing the Homosexual," *Commentary,* (December 1987).

side heterosexual men and women. As Maggie Gallagher notes, "We have not always been so woefully dependent upon the sexual act itself. Two hundred years ago, for example, homosexuality did not exist. There was sodomy, of course, and buggery, and fornication and adultery and other sexual sins, but none of these forbidden acts fundamentally altered the sexual landscape. A man who committed sodomy may have lost his soul, but he did not lose his gender. He did not become a homosexual, a third sex. That was the invention of the nineteenth-century imagination."[2]

The new notions of sexual *identity,* later sexual *preference,* and now sexual *orientation* have pervasively shaped the current cultural debate. Indeed, this was the ideological wedge used to force the American Psychiatric Association to remove homosexuality from the *Diagnostic and Statistical Manual of Mental Disorders* in 1973. It is still the most effective tactical concept employed in the debate. The politically useful concept of orientation is thus a trophy of the "triumph of the therapeutic," which has seen psychosocial arguments seize the popular consciousness.

---

2. Maggie Gallagher, *Enemies of Eros: How the Sexual Revolution Is Killing Family, Marriage, and Sex and What We Can Do About It* (Chicago: Bonus Books, 1989), 256–257.

Evangelicals must not allow this category to frame the debate. We cannot allow persons to be reduced to any sexual "orientation" as the defining characteristic of their identity. If the idea of orientation is based in reality, then what is its cause? Biological destiny? Genetic factors? Cultural conditioning? Parental influence? Environmental factors?

No adequate scientific data exists to prove any one of these—or any combination thereof—as the source of homosexual orientation. It is important to note that the hypothesis preceded any scientific proof, and yet it has been accepted as virtually self-evident. Evangelicals must reject the category as a therapeutic construct employed for ideological and political ends.

While it is not necessary for evangelicals to resist all scientific research, science is often enslaved to ideological agendas, as has been evident in some scientists' recent claims to have established a genetic basis for homosexuality. Evangelicals tend to overreact to such reports, some accepting the claims at face value and others running scared as if science could by genetic research overthrow the moral structure. Neither response is proper. Evangelicals should look critically at such research and carefully consider its unsubstantiated claims.

Yet we must avoid the overreaction which implies

that such research—even if verified to the satisfaction of all—would subvert God's command. The Christian understanding of sexual morality is not based on scientific grounds, and it is not open to scientific interrogation or investigation. Scientists cannot discover anything that can call into question the authority of God's command.

A genetic basis—unlikely in the extreme—would, even if objectively established, not carry great theological import. A genetic link may be established for any number of behaviors and patterns, but this does not diminish the moral significance of those acts nor the responsibility of the individual. After all, genetic links have been claimed for everything from diabetes and alcoholism to patterns of watching television.

We must also be careful to make clear that while we reject the concept of sexual orientation as a category of identity, we are not denying that there are some persons who discover themselves to be sexually attracted to persons of the same sex. Since our sexuality is such an important part of our lives, we are naturally tempted to think that our profile of sexual attraction is central to our identity. But our identity must not be constituted by mere sexuality. We are first of all human beings created in the image of God. Secondly, we are sinners whose fallenness is demonstrated in every aspect of our lives—including our sexuality.

Every single human being who has reached puberty has to deal with some kind of sexual temptation. For some, that profile of temptation is homosexual; for others it is heterosexual. The key issue for both is what God commands concerning our stewardship of sexuality and the gift of sex.

Evangelicals must reject the therapeutic construct and yet point to a biblical model. I believe that the lack of a mature biblical model for understanding homosexuality has diminished our ability to sustain a consistent moral argument in an adversarial culture. We must continue to bear faithful witness to the clear biblical injunctions concerning homosexual acts, that such acts are not only inherently sinful but also an abomination before the Lord. But the evangelical approach must be far more comprehensive, for the Bible is itself more comprehensive in approach. Scripture does not address mere homosexual acts; it communicates God's design for all of human sexuality, and thus provides a basis for understanding the implications of homosexuality for the family, society, and the church.

First, as Romans 1 makes absolutely clear, homosexuality is an act of unbelief. As Paul writes, the wrath of God is revealed against all those "who suppress the truth in unrighteousness" (verse 18). God has endowed all humanity with the knowledge of the Creator, and all are without excuse. Paul continues, "For they exchanged the truth of God for a lie, and worshiped and served the creature rather than the Creator, who is blessed forever. Amen. For this reason, God gave them over to degrading passions; for the women exchanged the natural function for that which is unnatural, and in the same way also the men abandoned the natural function of the woman and burned in their desire toward one another, men with men committing indecent acts and receiving in their own persons the due penalty of their error" (verses 25–27).

The broader context of Paul's rejection of homosexuality is clear: homosexuality is a dramatic sign of rebellion against God's sovereign intention in creation and a gross perversion of God's good and perfect plan for His created order. Those about whom Paul writes have worshiped the creature rather than the Creator. Thus, men and women have forfeited the natural complementarity of God's intention for heterosexual marriage and have turned to members of their own sex, burning with a desire which in itself is degrading and dishonorable. The logical progression in Romans 1 is undeniable. Paul shifts immediately from his description of rebellion against God as Creator to an identification of homosexuality—among both men and women—as the first and most evident sign of a society upon which God has turned His judgment.

Essential to understanding this reality in theological perspective is a recognition that homosexuality is an assault upon the integrity of creation and God's intention in creating human beings in two distinct and complementary genders. Here the confessing church runs counter to the spirit of the age. Even to raise the issue of gender is to offend those who wish to eradicate any gender distinctions by arguing that these are merely "socially constructed realities," vestiges of patriarchal past.

Scripture will not allow this attempt to deny the structures of creation. Romans 1 must be read in light of Genesis 1 and 2. As Genesis 1:27 makes apparent, God intended from the beginning to create human beings in two genders—"male and female He created them." Both man and woman were created in the image of God. They were distinct and yet inseparably linked by God's design. The genders were different, and the distinction transcended mere physical differences, but the man recognized in the woman "bone of my bones, and flesh of my flesh" (2:23).

The text does not stop with the mere creation of woman. Rather, God's creative intention is further revealed in the joining of the man to the woman. This bond between man and woman was marriage. Immediately following the creation of man and woman come the instructive words: "For this reason a man shall leave his father and his mother, and be joined to his wife; and they shall become one flesh. And the man and his wife were both naked and were not ashamed" (verses 24–25). This biblical assertion, which no revisionist exegesis can deconstruct, clearly places marriage and sexual relations within God's creative act and design.

Few theologians have given this critical issue its due attention. Indeed, throughout the history of the church, this pattern was seen as axiomatic and unquestioned. Only in the modern period, when social experimentation and radical protest movements have sought to push a wide-scale rejection of this pattern, has the issue come to light. Significantly, it is Karl Barth who has most seriously addressed this biblical pattern of gender complementarity. Writing in 1928, Barth asserted, "What do we really know about the male and female except that the male could not be a man without the female nor the female without the male, that the male cannot belong to himself without also belonging to the female and vice-versa?" In other words, the male and female only have meaning in relation to the other. Barth refers to Genesis 2:25 and suggests that the man and the woman saw each other naked and were not ashamed "because the maleness of the male and the femaleness of the female rightly become an object of shame...only when the male and female in their maleness and femaleness seek to belong to themselves and not to each other."

Horribly confused, the sexes turn inward to an "ideal of a masculinity free from woman and a femininity free from man," Barth asserted. This false ideal, which is a rejection of the Creator and His command, culminates in "the corrupt emotional and finally physical desire in which—in a sexual union which is not and cannot be genuine—man thinks that he must seek and can find in man, and woman in woman, a substitute for the despised partner."

Barth, writing in the first decades of the twentieth century, saw the coming challenge. His response remains prophetic, but it was unfinished. Carl F. H. Henry, perhaps the most significant figure in the development of evangelical theology in the last half century, rightly rejected Barth's extrabiblical theorizing and "fanciful exegesis" of the relation between sexual issues and the *imago dei*. Nonetheless, he agreed on this essential point: "The plurality of human existence is not optional; man cannot properly be man without speaking of male and female."[3]

The revolt against this divinely established order is one of the most important developments of the twentieth century, and it looms as one of the defining issues of the cultural revolution. Evangelicals must lay bare this assault upon creation, and yet do so in a way that is tied inextricably to biblical foundations, and not to cultural assumptions, however comfortable they may seem to secular society.

3. Carl F. H. Henry, *God, Revelation, and Authority,* Vol. 6 (Wheaton, IL: Crossway, 1999), 242.

9

HOMOSEXUALITY IN THEOLOGICAL PERSPECTIVE

Responding to the Challenge

How will evangelicals respond to the challenge of the homosexual movement? And how will the evangelical church respond to those persons struggling with homosexuality? These are critical questions that, when answered, will indicate the larger direction of the evangelical movement.

First, evangelicals must establish our understanding of homosexuality on the Bible and rest upon an undiluted affirmation of biblical authority. The Bible is unambiguous on the issue of homosexuality, and only a repudiation of biblical truth can allow evangelicals to join the moral revisionists. Our only authority for addressing this issue is that of God as revealed in holy Scripture. We can speak only because we are confident that the one sovereign God and Lord has revealed Himself and His will in an inerrant and authoritative Scripture. On the basis of that revelation, we cannot fail to speak and to confront the spirits of the age. Furthermore, we do so with confidence that the Christian claim to truth in the incarnation of the Son and the inscripturation of divine revelation is superior to any other claim to authority. Christians must neither cringe nor cavil in the face of secularism and its ideological manifestations. We must deconstruct the deconstructionists, turn the hermeneutic of suspicion upon the revisionists, and bear undiluted witness to the gospel and the Christian worldview. Therefore, we speak about homosexuality because we speak on the basis of divinely revealed truth. Our own ideas and conceptions of homosexuality are not authoritative. Our duty is to understand the mind and intention of God.

At this point we must address another evangelical temptation. A growing number of evangelicals are shifting the debate over homosexuality by attempting to base their arguments on natural law. Their motive is clear. The assumption is that natural-law reasoning will carry greater and broader cultural influence than arguments based explicitly upon divine revelation. The problem must be admitted. Explicitly theological arguments are increasingly declared off-limits for cultural and political discourse. The dominant media culture and legislative processes seem impervious to moral discourse rooted in the Christian worldview. Perhaps, it is argued, natural law will provide a *via media,* a middle way between secularism and theism.

Evangelicals must, of course, affirm both general revelation and the existence of natural law. God has most certainly revealed Himself in intelligible ways through the created order and the human conscience. But as Paul made so clear in Romans 1, the knowledge imparted by this authentic natural revelation is sufficient to damn but not to save. Christianity bases its claim upon special revelation in both holy Scriptures and the Incarnate Son, Jesus the Christ. The moral order God has implanted in His creation is tangible, evident, and undeniable. Yet in contemporary America, as in Paul's discussion in Romans, human beings reject that knowledge and suffer the consequences.

My warning on this issue is twofold. First, to revert

to natural-law reasoning is to retreat from the high ground of the Christian truth claim. In order to meet secular demands, the church would shift its argument from the unassailable ground of holy Scripture to the contested terrain of nature and the cosmos.

This is what, in another context, F. A. Hayek termed "a fatal conceit." From such an abdication there is no recovery. Though evangelicals and conservative Roman Catholics will find themselves compatriots in the cultural struggle, it is not possible for evangelicals to adopt natural-law reasoning as a basis for moral argumentation and remain authentically evangelical. Natural-law reasoning may provide a point of conversation and serve as a means of introducing the revealed law, but it cannot stand as a mode of evangelical moral discourse and reasoning.

For some, it may seem that a step back from the special revelation of the positive law (as compared to natural law) would be justified as a means to a greater end. Once a consensus or point of contact with the secular culture has been established, it is claimed, the discussion can be shifted to positive law and the Christian worldview. This raises the pragmatic warning: this strategy does not work.

The cultural elites and the generations raised in the

aftermath of the sexual revolution are no more moved by natural-law arguments than by explicitly Christian assertions. Natural-law reasoning is no more welcome in Congress or among the media than a recitation of the Ten Commandments. Furthermore, there is no common understanding in elite circles as to what the natural law would require. A reflection on the congressional hearings for the confirmations of Robert Bork and Clarence Thomas should make this reality abundantly clear. Natural-law arguments are not culturally compelling.

Evangelicals should not hesitate to *illustrate* arguments from Scripture with allusions to nature and the natural order. But the order of ethical reasoning is critical: evangelicals can turn to nature as illustration *after* basing the moral argument on Scripture. At its best, the evangelical temptation to turn to natural-law reasoning is an attempt in a difficult cultural context to establish a moral consensus. But this strategy will not succeed. At its worst, this temptation represents a repudiation of the gospel and an abdication of evangelical faith.

We must minister to homosexuals from the full wealth of Christian conviction and knowledge. Evangelical Christians have often failed at this task. We have talked carelessly about homosexuality and have said at times both too little and too much. We must make clear the fact that we know *all* persons to be sinners— even sexual sinners. There is no one beyond the age of puberty who is not a sexual sinner.

We must also learn to speak honestly to those who struggle with same-sex sexual attractions. We must stop telling them that they have *chosen* this pattern of temptation. They do not believe this, and indeed they have not chosen this temptation in itself. They—and we— are nevertheless fully accountable for what we *do* about sexual temptation. We are also fully accountable for our willingness to feed temptation and to learn to enjoy it. We are further accountable for attempts to rationalize our sin as something other than what it is.

Regardless of the pattern of sexual temptation, the only way out of the problem is redemption in Christ. No act of the will, no matter how titanic, can solve the problem of sin or offer liberty from the prison of our temptations. The only way out is through the redemption Christ has accomplished. The only way to deal with the problem of sin is to trust the transforming power of the gospel and the renewal that comes to the believer in Christ. Even then, struggle with sexual temptation will persist—but not without hope and healing.

Finally, our trust must be in the Sovereign God who is the Creator and Sustainer of all. He and He alone holds the prerogative to define and limit sexuality. It is one of His good gifts to His creatures, which they, in their rebellion, have contorted and degraded. Evangelicals must affirm that God has defined sexuality and that our duty is to follow His command. This means that evangelical Christians must with increased effectiveness uphold the biblical model of sexuality. We must affirm its goodness without embarrassment, give thanks for the gift and its enjoyment, acknowledge without hesitation that God intended sexual relations for pleasure as well as for procreation, and never retreat from the clear biblical teaching that sex is intended only for the context of committed and monogamous heterosexual marriage. This model of sexual wholeness, lived daily in the lives of millions of families and couples, will bear eloquent testimony before the world— even when it is ridiculed.

We must learn to address the issue of homosexuality and other difficult sexual issues with candor, directness, and unembarrassed honesty. This is not an hour for prudish denial. To fail at the task of speaking clearly and directly to this issue is to fail to speak where God has spoken. We must also acknowledge that the only inhibiting force in the world which limits the range and extent of sexual perversion is common grace. But for the continuing presence of common grace, the world would slide into even more degraded darkness. For that grace we must be thankful.

But the issue of homosexuality affords a unique opportunity for the confessing church to bear witness to particular grace as well, to give witness to the gospel as the only means of salvation and of Jesus Christ as the sole and sufficient Savior. Salvation and repentance must be preached to homosexuals—and to heterosexuals as well. East of Eden, not one of us has come before God as sexually pure and whole, even if we have never committed an illicit sexual act. Our ministry to homosexuals is not as the sinless ministering to sinners, but as fellow sinners who bear testimony to the reality of salvation through faith in Jesus Christ.

The gospel always comes as both judgment and grace. But the last word must always be grace. Our duty is to tell the truth about homosexuality and to name it as Scripture names it. But our responsibility hardly ends there, for our next task is to speak the word of grace, and to present the gospel of salvation by grace through faith in Christ as our substitute, by whose blood we have been bought with a price.

To the homosexual, as to all others, we must speak

in love, never in hatred. But the first task of love is to tell the truth, and the sign of true hatred is the telling of a lie. Those who genuinely love homosexuals are not those who would revolutionize morality to meet their wishes, but those who will tell them the truth and point them to the One who is the way, the truth, and the life (see John 14:6).

10

THE END OF FRIENDSHIP

How Sexual Confusion Has Tainted Friendship Between Men

A Hollywood movie became something of a flashpoint in America's culture war in 2005. Though it opened in only three cities and was not exactly a blockbuster at the box office, *Brokeback Mountain,* starring Heath Ledger and Jake Gyllenhaal as two cowboys linked in a homosexual romance, was critically acclaimed and exhaustively covered in the nation's media. The Academy of Motion Picture Arts and Sciences awarded it three Oscars in 2006, including Best

Achievement in Directing and Best Writing for an Adapted Screenplay.

Directed by Ang Lee, *Brokeback Mountain* is based on a short story of the same title by author Annie Proulx. The story is quite graphic, depicting an unexpected homosexual romance between two cowboys who find themselves alone in a tent. As the story unfolds, the homosexual relationship is continued even as the two men get married and establish families. Both the story and the movie include explicit sex and depict the hurt and turmoil experienced by the families of these two men as they periodically take what are described as "fishing trips in which there is no fishing." Nevertheless, the movie presents the homosexual romance as a relationship to be admired—insinuating that if our society could be freed of its hang-ups about homosexuality, these two could have gone on to live together happily ever after.

In one sense, the real significance of *Brokeback Mountain* doesn't have anything to do with cinematography. Instead, it has everything to do with our culture and the breakdown of sexual order. *Brokeback Mountain* represents something new in mainstream America—a celebration of homosexual romance on the big screen. The very fact that this movie stars two relatively well-established young actors and has drawn the fawning attention of Hollywood critics indicates that something very serious is afoot. It really does not matter that most Americans did not see this film. Now that this cultural barrier has been broken down, depictions of similar relationships and romances are sure to filter down into popular entertainment—and quickly.

Anthony Esolen, professor of English at Providence College in Providence, Rhode Island, warns that this breakdown of the natural sexual order has led to the death of friendship—particularly to the death of male friendships.

In "A Requiem for Friendship: Why Boys Will Not Be Boys and Other Consequences of the Sexual Revolution," published in the September 2005 issue of *Touchstone* magazine,[1] Esolen begins by reminding readers of a scene from J. R. R. Tolkien's great work *The Lord of the Rings.* Sam Gamgee, having followed his master Frodo into Mordor, the realm of death, finds him in a small filthy cell lying half conscious. "Frodo! Mr. Frodo, my dear!" Sam cries. "It's Sam, I've come!" Frodo embraces his friend and Sam eventually cradles

---

1. Anthony Esolen, "A Requiem for Friendship: Why Boys Will Not Be Boys and Other Consequences of the Sexual Revolution," *Touchstone* (September 2005). Used with permission.

Frodo's head. As Esolen suggests, a reader or viewer of this scene is likely to jump to a rather perverse conclusion: "What, are they gay?"

Esolen suggests that this question is an "ignorant but inevitable response" to the context. He goes on to recall that Shakespeare and many other great authors spoke of nonsexual love between men in strongest terms. Similarly, when David is told of the death of his friend Jonathan, he cries, "Your love to me was more wonderful than the love of women" (2 Samuel 1:26).

As Esolen understands, the corruption of language has contributed to this confusion. When words like *love, friend, male, female,* and *partner* are transformed in a new sexual context, what was once understood to be pure and undefiled is now subject to sniggering and disrespect. Esolen insists that this linguistic shift was no accident. He accuses "pansexualists" of corrupting the language in order to normalize sexual confusion and anarchy. They have used language "as a tool for establishing their own order and imposing it on everyone else," he argues. As Esolen explains, "The pansexualists—they who believe in the libertarian dogma that what two consenting adults do with their privates in private is nobody's business—understand that the language had to be changed to assist the realization of their dream, and also that the realization of their dream would change the world, because it would change the language for everyone else."

What does all this have to do with *Brokeback Mountain*? "Open homosexuality, loudly and defiantly celebrated, changes the language for everyone," Esolen insists. "If a man throws his arm around another man's waist, it is now a sign—whether he is on the political right or the left, whether he believes in biblical proscriptions of homosexuality or not." Esolen offers a blunt and haunting assessment: "If a man cradles the head of his weeping friend, the shadow of suspicion must cross your mind."

One of the words and realities most clearly corrupted for the sake of sexual anarchy is *friendship*—and male friendship in particular. "For modern American men, friendship is no longer forged in the heat of battle, or in the dust of the plains as they drive their herds across half a continent, or in the choking air of a coalmine, or even in the cigar smoke of a debating club," Esolen notes. Most men no longer find themselves in situations that encourage and inculcate straightforward male friendships. As Esolen observes, "The sexual revolution has also nearly killed male friendship as devoted to anything beyond drinking and watching sports; and the homosexual movement, a logically inevitable result of forty years of heterosexual promiscuity and feminist folly, bids fair to finish it off and nail the coffin shut."

What this means for grown men is bad enough, but Esolen is persuasive when he argues that the most vulnerable victims of friendship's demise are boys. "The prominence of male homosexuality changes the language for teenage boys. It is absurd and cruel to say that the boy can ignore it. Even if he would, his classmates will not let him. All boys need to prove that they are not failures. They need to prove that they are on the way to becoming men—that they are not going to relapse into the need to be protected by, and therefore identified with, their mothers." So? Esolen argues that boys, deprived of normal recognitions of masculinity and safe friendships with other boys and men, often turn to aggressive sexual promiscuity with girls in order to prove that they are not homosexual. Boys who refuse to play this game are tagged as homosexuals.

Esolen is on to something of incredible importance here. He reminds us all that boys need the uncomplicated camaraderie of other boys in order to negotiate their own path to manhood. The friendships shared among boys and young men allowed them to come together around common interests and activities and to channel their natural curiosity and energy into participation in shared activities. As young males band together, Esolen acknowledges that they "might do a thousand things fascinatingly creative and dangerously destructive." This is where adults must step in to guide these energies in positive directions and to erect boundaries to prevent or discourage bad behavior. In any event, these boys would not, as Esolen argues many boys do now, stagnate. "They would be alive," he asserts.

All this requires an uncomplicated heterosexual expectation. Esolen points to the fact that Abraham Lincoln, as a young man, had often shared a bed with his friend Joshua Speed. The two men shared letters that spoke of their appreciation and love for each other. Modern readers have jumped to the conclusion that Lincoln must have been a homosexual. Esolen rightly argues that this "evidence" proves exactly the opposite. Lincoln and Speed were free to share a bed together, and to speak of their deep friendship, precisely because they did not fear any revelation of this fact or of their relationship to the public. Why? Because the nearly universal understanding of all homosexual behavior as immoral and deviant created a context in which *no one* would have had the expectation that Lincoln would be involved in homosexuality. As Esolen explains, "The stigma against sodomy cleared away ample space for an emotionally powerful friendship that did not involve sexual intercourse, exactly as the stigma against incest allows for the physical and emotional freedom of a family."

In a truly haunting section of his essay, Esolen asked us to imagine a society in which the taboo against incest has been removed. Under such circumstances, no uncle would be free to hug his young niece without an accusation of sexual interest. Relationships between parents and children, brothers and sisters, and relatives of all varieties would be corrupted and undermined by the imposition of sexual suspicion.

As Esolen understands, this is exactly what is happening as homosexuality is normalized in the culture. Normal, nonsexual, fraternal friendships among men now come under suspicion. This is especially true for teenage boys and young men, who are less secure about their manhood and more concerned about their own—and their peers'—sexual identities.

The normalization of homosexuality destroys the natural order of friendships among men. "Think about that friendship, the next time you see the perpetual adolescents in feather boas as they march down Main Street, making their sexual proclivities known to everybody whether everybody cares or not," Esolen instructs. "With every chanted slogan and every blaring sign, they crowd out the words of friendship, they appropriate the healthy gestures of love between man and man. Confess—has it not left you uneasy even to read the words of that last sentence?"

Of course, we are told that those who hold such concerns are simply providing evidence of their innate homophobia and repressive sexual hang-ups. The critics will celebrate *Brokeback Mountain,* and we can now expect a flood of similar themes, stories, and depictions. Society at large is corrupted by the normalization of homosexuality, and the bonds of normal male friendships are weakened, if not destroyed. Remember all this as Hollywood celebrates its latest cultural "achievement."

_____ **11**

AFTER THE BALL

Why the Homosexual
Movement Has Won

The spectacular success of the homosexual movement stands as one of the most fascinating phenomena of our time. In less than two decades, homosexuality has moved from "the love that dares not
speak its name" to the center of America's public life.
The homosexual agenda has advanced even more
quickly than its most ardent proponents had expected,
and social change of this magnitude demands some
explanation.

A partial explanation of the homosexual movement's success can be traced to the 1989 publication of
After the Ball: How America Will Conquer Its Fear and

Hatred of Gays in the 90's. Published with little fanfare, this book became the authoritative public relations manual for the homosexual agenda, and its authors presented the book as a distillation of public relations advice for the homosexual community. A look back at its pages is an occasion for understanding just how successful their plan was.

Authors Marshall Kirk and Hunter Madsen combined psychiatric and public relations expertise in devising their strategy. Kirk, a researcher in neuropsychiatry, and Madsen, a public relations consultant, argued that homosexuals must change their presentation to the heterosexual community if real success was to be made. Conceiving their book as a "gay manifesto for the 1990s," the authors called for homosexuals to repackage themselves as mainstream citizens demanding equal treatment, rather than as a promiscuous sexual minority seeking greater opportunity and influence. Writing just as the AIDS crisis hit its greatest momentum, the authors saw the disease as an opportunity to change the public mind. "As cynical as it may seem, AIDS gives us a chance, however brief, to establish ourselves as a victimized minority legitimately deserving of America's special protection and care," they wrote.

Give them credit: they really did understand the

operation of the public mind. Kirk and Madsen called for homosexuals to talk incessantly in public about homosexuality. "Open, frank talk makes gayness seem less furtive, alien, and sinful; more above board," they asserted. "Constant talk builds the impression that public opinion is at least divided on the subject, and that a sizeable bloc—the most modern, up-to-date citizens—accept or even practice homosexuality." Nevertheless, not all talk about homosexuality is helpful. "In the early stages of the campaign, the public should not be shocked and repelled by premature exposure to homosexual behavior itself." Rather, the issue would be presented as a question of rights, laws, and prejudices—in short, homosexuality would be reduced to "an abstract social question."

Portraying homosexuals as victims was essential to their strategy. Offering several principles for tactical advance in their cause, the authors called upon homosexuals to portray themselves as victims of society, not as revolutionaries. If straights came to see gays as oppressed sufferers, they would eventually be "inclined by reflex to adopt the role of protector." Such a strategy could, they asserted, lead to something like a "conversion" of the public mind on the question of homosexuality. "The purpose of victim imagery is to make straights feel very uncomfortable," they explained. In time, straights might actually tire of feeling like oppressors, come to sympathize with gays, and even feel compelled to help them reverse the injustice society had inflicted on them.

Obviously, this would mean marginalizing some members of the homosexual community. Kirk and Madsen were bold to advise a mainstreaming of the homosexual image. "Cocky mustachioed leather-men, drag queens, and bull dykes" could not be the public face of the movement. Attractive young people, middle-aged women, well-appointed professionals, and smiling seniors would be far more likely to generate the needed sympathy. Furthermore, the most extreme gay groups, such as NAMBLA [North American Man/Boy Love Association], would have to be kept out of the public eye completely. As Kirk and Madsen acknowledged, "Suspected child molesters will never look like victims."

What about the origin of sexual orientation? The success of the homosexual movement can be largely traced to the very idea of "orientation" itself. More precisely, homosexuals advanced their cause by arguing that they were born that way. Madsen and Kirk offer this as candid public relations advice: "Gays should be considered to have been born gay." Alas, "To suggest in public that homosexuality might be chosen is to open the can of worms labeled 'moral choices and sin' and give the religious intransigents a stick to beat us with. Straights must be taught that it is as natural for some persons to be homosexual as it is for others to be heterosexual: wickedness and seduction have nothing to do with it."

There can be no doubt that Christianity represents the greatest obstacle to the normalization of homosexual behavior. It cannot be otherwise, because of the clear biblical teachings concerning the inherent sinfulness of homosexuality in all forms and the normativity of heterosexual marriage. In order to counter this obstacle, Kirk and Madsen advised gays to "use talk to muddy the moral waters" by publicizing the support of liberal churches, challenging traditional interpretations of biblical teaching, and even arguing that Christian teaching on sexuality is itself characterized by "inconsistency and hatred." Conservative churches, defined by the authors as "homohating" are portrayed as "antiquated backwaters, badly out of step with the times and with the latest findings of psychology."

Other principles offered by the authors included making gays look good by identifying strategic historical figures as being hidden homosexuals and, on the other hand, making "victimizers" look bad in the public eye. Kirk and Madsen suggested isolating conservative Christians by presenting them as "hysterical backwoods preachers, drooling with hate to a degree that looks both comical and deranged." They offered a concrete example of how this strategy could be used on television and in print. "For example, for several seconds an unctuous beady-eyed Southern preacher is shown pounding the pulpit in rage against 'those perverted, abominable creatures.' While his tirade continues over the soundtrack, the picture switches to heart-rending photos of badly beaten persons, or of gays who look decent, harmless, and likeable; and then we cut back to the poisonous face of the preacher. The contrast speaks for itself. The effect is devastating."

A quick review of the last fifteen years demonstrates the incredible effectiveness of this public-relations advice. The agenda set out by Kirk and Madsen led to nothing less than social transformation. By portraying themselves as mainstream Americans seeking nothing but liberty and self-fulfillment, homosexuals redefined the moral equation. Issues of right and wrong were isolated as outdated, repressive, and culturally embarrassing. Instead, the assertion of "rights" became the hallmark of the public relations strategy.

No doubt public relations is now a major part of the American economy, with hundreds of millions of dollars poured into advertising strategies and image enhancement programs. Observers of the public-relations world must look back with slack-jawed amazement at the phenomenal success of the approach undertaken by homosexuals over the last two decades. The advice offered by Marshall Kirk and Hunter Madsen is nothing less than a manifesto for moral revolution. A look back at this strategy indicates just how self-consciously the homosexual movement advanced its cause by following this plan.

Those who oppose the normalization of homosexuality have indeed been presented as backwoods, antiquated, and dangerous people, while those advancing the cause are presented as forces for light, progress, and acceptance. Conservative Christians have been presented as proponents of hatred rather than as individuals driven by biblical conviction. The unprecedented success of this public-relations strategy helps to explain everything from why America has accepted homosexual characters and plotlines in prime-time entertainment to the lack of outrage in response to same-sex marriage in Massachusetts.

At least we know what we are up against. Biblical

Christians must continue to talk about right and wrong even when the larger world dismisses morality as an outdated concept. We must maintain marriage as a nonnegotiable norm—a union of a man and a woman—even when the courts redefine marriage by fiat. At the same time, we must take into account the transformation of the American mind that is now so devastatingly evident to all who have eyes to see.

The real tragedy of *After the Ball* is that the great result of this is not a party but the complete rejection of the very moral foundations that made this society possible. In order to address the most fundamental problems, we must understand the shape of the American mind. Looking back at *After the Ball* after fifteen years, it all comes into frightening focus.

12

ALFRED KINSEY

The Man as He Really Was

In 2004, the movie *Kinsey* introduced a new generation of Americans to the infamous "father" of sex research in America. Yet, the movie was really not a true portrait of Alfred Kinsey at all. Instead of portraying the twisted and tormented mind of this propagandist for the sexual revolution, it presented Kinsey as an angel of light who brought America out of repression and darkness.

Reviewers greeted the movie with excitement. A. O. Scott, writing in the *New York Times,* declared the movie a "smart, stirring life" and praised it for treating the subject of sex with "sobriety, sensitivity and a welcome measure of humor." Scott neglects to mention that the movie treats its subject without an adequate measure of truth.

Rather than expressing outrage that a scandalous individual with a well-documented pattern of sexual perversity is being celebrated, Scott sees the movie as a mixture of entertainment and enlightenment. "I can't think of another movie," he gushed, "that has dealt with sex so knowledgeably and, at the same time, made the pursuit of knowledge seem so sexy. There are some explicit images and provocative scenes, but it is your intellect that is most likely to be aroused."

The reviewers for *Newsweek* acknowledged that "Kinsey's methods were far from perfect," but they nevertheless celebrated both the movie and its central character. Indeed, they commend Kinsey, who, they say, "shattered any vestiges of Victorian modesty, leading curious Americans from bedroom peephole to up-front view between the sheets." In a sidebar, David Ansen declared that the movie "is a celebration of diversity; it's about the solace knowledge can bring." Writing in the *Wall Street Journal,* reviewer Joe Morgenstern declared that *Kinsey* doesn't try to sell or exploit sex. According to Morgenstern, the movie "does remarkably well as a cultural history of a vanished time" and "is intelligent to a fault."

Alfred C. Kinsey is one of the most controversial figures in American history—and for good reason. An entomologist by training, Kinsey turned from his intense fascination with the gall wasp to the study of human sexuality. He burst upon the American scene with his pioneering 1948 volume *Sexual Behavior in the Human Male*. Eventually, Indiana University was to establish the Kinsey Institute for Research in Sex, Gender, and Reproduction, and the name "Kinsey" would be associated with progressivist sex education, opposition to traditional sexual morality, and liberation from fixed concepts of "normal" when dealing with human sexuality. The Kinsey Institute has what many consider to be the world's largest collection of pornography, sexually explicit art, and various sexual objects. What the institute does not advertise is its links to data gathered by child molesters and sex criminals.

By any measure, Alfred Kinsey was a tormented and conflicted figure. Raised by a puritanical father and a withdrawn mother, Kinsey's adolescence was marked by sexual turmoil and experimentation. As is now well documented, the young Kinsey was involved in sadomasochistic sexual behaviors and was driven by homosexual desire.

In a groundbreaking biography published in 1997,

James H. Jones blew the cover on the Kinsey myth.[1] According to this popular and pervasive mythology, Alfred Kinsey was a scientist who brought his rigorous scientific skills and objective scientific interests to the study of human sexuality. The real Alfred Kinsey was a man whose own sexual practices cannot be safely described to the general public and whose interest in sex was anything but objective or scientific. From the onset, Jones recognized Kinsey's central role in the sexual revolution. "More than any other American of the twentieth century," Jones acknowledges, "he was the architect of a new sensibility about a part of life that everyone experiences and no one escapes." Nevertheless, the real Kinsey was hidden from the public. Jones describes his project in these words: "As I burrowed into more than a dozen archives, read tens of thousands of letters, and interviewed scores of people who knew Kinsey in various capacities, I discovered that his public image distorted more than it revealed."

As Jones reports, "The man I came to know bore no resemblance to the canonical Kinsey. Anything but disinterested, he approached his work with missionary

---

1. James H. Jones, *Alfred C. Kinsey: A Public/Private Life* (New York: W. W. Norton, 1997).

fervor. Kinsey loathed Victorian morality as only a person who had been badly injured by sexual repression could despise it. He was determined to use science to strip human sexuality of its guilt and repression. He wanted to undermine traditional morality, to soften the rules of restraint, and to help people develop positive attitudes toward their sexual needs and desires. Kinsey was a crypto-reformer who spent his every waking hour attempting to change the sexual mores and sex offender laws of the United States."

There was more to it than that, of course, and Jones marshals an incredible mountain of documentation to prove this point. In the first place, the adolescent Alfred Kinsey was deeply involved in masochistic self-abuse. In Jones's words, "Somewhere along the line, he veered off the path of normal development and was pulled down a trail that led to tremendous emotional conflict and self-negating physical abuse."

Driven by wild sexual fantasies and determined to overthrow what he saw as a repressive sexual morality, Kinsey eventually dropped his study of insects and turned his study to human sexuality. Tragically, Jones must acknowledge that the world of science "would have been better served had Kinsey not allowed his lust for data to obscure his judgment."

What exactly was Kinsey up to? He and his close band of young male associates went about collecting an enormous body of data on human sexuality, first looking at male, and later at female, populations. In his research on the sexual behavior of males, Kinsey brought his ideological and personal passions to the forefront of his supposedly scientific work. He arbitrarily decided that each human being could be located somewhere along a continuum of development between heterosexual and homosexual poles. He developed a six-step chart and argued that men and boys are arrayed all along this line between absolute heterosexuality and absolute homosexuality. He would later argue that almost 40 percent of all males would have some homosexual experience. Of course, hidden from public view was the fact that Kinsey was doing his very best to rationalize his own homosexuality—or bisexuality as later commentators would explain—and was not at all the objective scientist collecting neutral data from a responsible population base.

Among the many problems inherent in Kinsey's research is the fact that he relied upon reports and sexual studies taken from prison populations, including sex criminals. Therefore, Kinsey's notion of "normal" was drawn from a decidedly abnormal population sample.

The most troubling aspect of Kinsey's research is

the data he collected on the sexual response of children—especially young boys. Chapter 5 of *Sexual Behavior in the Human Male* considered the sexual experience of boys, including infants. Kinsey wanted to prove that children are sexual beings who should be understood to have and to deserve sexual experiences. In this chapter, Kinsey is largely depending upon the data contributed by "Mr. X," a man who had molested hundreds of boys ranging from infants to adolescents. As Jones explains, "Viewed from any angle, his relationship with Mr. X was a cautionary tale. Whatever the putative value as science of Mr. X's experience, the fact remains that he was a predator pedophile." Over decades, this man abused hundreds of young boys, tortured infants, and, as Jones explains, "performed a variety of other sexual acts on preadolescent boys and girls alike."

Kinsey did not condemn this man but instead eagerly solicited his "data." As a matter of fact, Kinsey went so far as to attempt to pay Mr. X for further research and once wrote to him, "I wish I knew how to give credit to you in the forthcoming volume for your material. It seems a shame not even to name you." Those words betray a moral monster of the most horrible depravity and assured criminality. Alfred Kinsey celebrated the fact that this man had sexually tortured children and, as Kinsey's own published work documents, had sexually abused two-month-old infants. All this was explicit in the data published in Kinsey's 1948 volume, but he was nonetheless celebrated as a sexual pioneer and as a prophet of sexual enlightenment.

Unbeknownst to the general public, Kinsey was also involved in sex acts with his staff and in the filming of hundreds of persons involved in sexual activity—including footage taken of his own masochistic sex acts. He and his colleagues paid adolescent boys to perform sex acts on film and turned the Kinsey house into a studio for pornographic documentation. In one incredibly weird twist on the story, Mrs. Kinsey, or "Mac" as she was known, is remembered to have brought refreshments to the participants at the conclusion of their sex acts and video sessions. She was herself filmed in various sexual situations, and Kinsey encouraged his associates to engage in sex acts with his wife.

What does the cultural elite now make of all this? The *New York Times* review acknowledged that the movie took a great risk "in attempting to deal frankly with its hero's own sex life without succumbing to prurience or easy moralism." In reality, however, the movie did not deal frankly with Kinsey's perversions at all. The reviewer concedes, "Sometimes his scientific zeal shaded into obsession, and his methods went from the empirical to the experimental in ways that remain ethically troubling." Ethically troubling? Is that all the *New York Times* can muster in response to Kinsey's own self-documented and published reports of child molestation?

In *Sex the Measure of All Things: A Life of Alfred C. Kinsey*, Jonathan Gathorne-Hardy laments the fact that Kinsey is not given the respect of his fellow scientists that he believed he deserved. Nevertheless, even Gathorne-Hardy acknowledges, "The recent digging up of Kinsey's private life, incidentally, is not going to help him" in this respect. Gathorne-Hardy wrote his book largely in response to the damage to Kinsey's reputation inflicted by Jones's biography. Amazingly, Gathorne-Hardy claims, "Wherever we know something of his sexuality it is at once apparent that, while it hardly ever, if ever, impaired his integrity as a scientist, it had a decisive effect on his work. And where it does once or twice seem to impair that integrity, the effect is either not very significant—or else it is obvious. There is a transparency." This is moral nonsense. Of course, this author attempts to make lemonade out of Kinsey's lemons in more than one way. At one point, Gathorne-Hardy goes so far as to claim that Kinsey's bisexuality was a great asset for his scientific work. "Kinsey was bi-sexual," Gathorne-Hardy notes, "an almost ideal position, one might think, for someone who was studying sexual behavior in both sexes." Exactly who might think this?

We have become a society that celebrates men like Alfred C. Kinsey and produces movies that present such a man as an agent of enlightenment, rather than as a tortured soul fighting his internal demons while soliciting data on the sexual molestation of young children—and filming any number of persons involved in any number of perverted sex acts.

In a letter he once wrote to his associate Clarence A. Tripp, Kinsey conceded, "The whole army of religion is our central enemy." Kinsey knew what he was up against, and his ambition was not merely to collect data but to overthrow the entire structure of Christian morality in the realm of human sexuality. Instead of being rightly classified as a criminal along with the likes of Dr. Joseph Mengele and other Nazi scientists, Alfred C. Kinsey is now lionized and celebrated in a movie starring Liam Neeson as the supposedly heroic figure. What does this say about Liam Neeson? What does this say about us?

13

MOURNING GAY CULTURE

The Riddle of Andrew Sullivan

A ndrew Sullivan is a man of ideas. In recent years, Sullivan has emerged as one of the most influential intellectuals in American public life. Furthermore, he has been identified with some of the most controversial issues of our times—a fact that is hardly surprising given his libertarian view of morality, conservative views of politics, Roman Catholic views of Christianity, and the fact that he is a prominent homosexual advocate.

Sullivan came to national and international attention as editor of the *New Republic* from 1991 to 1996.

He came to this post after earning degrees at Oxford University (BA) and Harvard University (PhD). Under his editorship, the *New Republic* became known as one of the nation's most lively, informative, and controversial journals of opinion. The courage and imagination demonstrated in Sullivan's editorship is the most likely explanation for the controversy that brought his downfall as editor. Nevertheless, Sullivan continues to contribute to the magazine as a senior editor.

In the October 24, 2005, issue of the *New Republic,* Sullivan writes about "The End of Gay Culture." Of course, Sullivan's perspective on homosexuality and gay culture is deeply rooted in his own homosexuality and his ardent embrace of his own homosexual lifestyle. He is anything but a dispassionate observer. In this article, Sullivan describes the massive transformation of American culture we are all now observing, at least in terms of the rapid normalization of homosexuality in public culture. Sullivan sees this as a two-edged sword for homosexuals.

On the one hand, the assimilation of homosexuals and homosexuality into the larger culture means that homosexuals are no longer outsiders. On the other hand, Sullivan sees the demise of a gay subculture as a significant loss, at least for the homosexuals who remember the experience of defining themselves by "transgressing" cultural norms. As evidence of this transformation, Sullivan points to his experience of almost two decades as a summer resident of Provincetown on Cape Cod. Over the last quarter century, Provincetown has become a mecca for gay men and lesbians, "a place where a separate identity essentially defines a separate place." Sullivan describes the Provincetown perspective: "No one bats an eye if two men walk down the street holding hands, or if a lesbian couple pecks each other on the cheek, or if a drag queen dressed as Cher careens down the main strip on a motor scooter." Nevertheless, that vision of Provincetown doesn't exist anymore, Sullivan explains. "As gay America has changed, so, too, has Provincetown. In a microcosm of what is happening across this country, its culture is changing."

The changes indicate that homosexuals in America no longer feel the need for a separate identity, a separate place, and a separate lifestyle. A real-estate boom has turned Provincetown into a resort for wealthy homosexuals where class is now more important than sexuality. Furthermore, the domesticization of homosexual culture has also changed the picture: "The number of children of gay couples has soared, and, some weeks, strollers clog the sidewalks." Beyond this, "week after week this summer, couple after couple got married—well over a thousand in the year and a half since gay marriage has been legal in Massachusetts."

As he sees it, America is no longer marked by a "single gay identity." Instead, a proliferation of niche sexual identities and cultures has replaced the dominant gay ethos that emerged in the 1970s. "Slowly but unmistakably, gay culture is ending," Sullivan observes. "In fact, it is beginning to dawn on many that the very concept of gay culture may one day disappear altogether." That is not to say that gay men and lesbians will cease to exist, or that homosexuality will no longer be present in society. Rather, it is to say that as gay culture continues to expand and become more and more mainstream, " 'gayness' alone will cease to tell you very much about any individual."

This is the world homosexuals have long dreamed of, Sullivan admits. Nevertheless, to let go of the idea of "distinctive gayness" is for many homosexuals "as hard as it is liberating, as saddening as it is invigorating."

Sullivan points to one central factor that explains the rapid transformation of American culture and its assimilation of homosexuals and homosexuality—the HIV epidemic. "The history of gay America," he says, is "defined by a plague that struck almost poignantly at the headiest moment of liberation. The entire structure of emergent gay culture—sexual, radical, subversive— met a virus that killed almost everyone it touched. Virtually the entire generation that pioneered gay culture was wiped out—quickly."

The HIV epidemic established homosexuality as a central cultural concern and, quite unexpectedly, served to normalize homosexuality within the culture. The HIV plague "established homosexuality as a legitimate topic more swiftly than any political manifesto could possibly have done," Sullivan asserts.

As he reviews the impact of the HIV crisis, Sullivan points to some patterns that emerged in its aftermath—patterns that would likely be missed by those outside the gay subculture. The emergence of lesbians as leaders of the major gay rights organizations was, Sullivan suggests, largely due to the fact that the gay male leaders were mostly dead. Thus, "It was only natural, perhaps, that the next generation of leaders tended to be lesbian." Moreover, Sullivan hints, but does not openly suggest, that lesbians were also successful in pushing a more domestic picture of homosexuality. The radical sexual promiscuity so common to many homosexual men was replaced, in the public eye, with the more settled picture of lesbian couples, often with children.

Meanwhile, a whole new generation was emerging—younger homosexuals who grew to maturity (or were even born) after the HIV epidemic. "For the first time," Sullivan observes, "a cohort of gay children and teens grew up in a world where homosexuality was no longer a taboo subject and where gay figures were regularly featured in the press." The younger generation seems to want homosexuality to be seen as normal, not exceptional. This is verified by the research published by Ritch C. Savin-Williams in his book *The New Gay Teenager.* Sullivan's generation, on the other hand, fears the loss of the more radical homosexual culture that emerged after events such as New York's Stonewall Rebellion and the rebranding of San Francisco's Castro district as a gay haven.

Sullivan's point is clear: the transition of homosexual culture represents the substitution of Ellen DeGeneres for the "bull-dykes" and "lipstick lesbians" of the past. Likewise, well-known homosexual male celebrities define homosexuality in the public culture, rather than "hyper-masculine bikers and muscle men." Sullivan admits (or celebrates) the fact that "these sub-sub-cultures still exist." Yet, "the polarities in the larger gay population are far less pronounced than they once were; the edges have softened."

In this article, Sullivan is returning to ground he has covered before. His 1995 book *Virtually Normal* described the struggle between "prohibitionists," "liberationists," "conservatives," and "liberals" in the homosexual community. During this period, Sullivan emerged as a major (and, at least at first, quite lonely) proponent of same-sex marriage. "Gay marriage is not a radical step," Sullivan insisted. "It is a profoundly humanizing, traditionalizing step. It is the first step in any resolution of the homosexual question—more important than any other institution, since it is the most central institution to the nature of the problem, which is to say, the emotional and sexual bond between one human being and another. If nothing else were done at all, and gay marriage were legalized, ninety percent of the political work necessary to achieve gay and lesbian equality would have been achieved. It is ultimately the only reform that truly matters." But, even as Sullivan argued for the acceptance and legalization of same-sex marriage, more radical homosexual theorists were dismissing marriage altogether. As Sullivan explained, "Marriage of all institutions is to liberationists a form of imprisonment; it reeks of a discourse that has bought and sold property, that has denigrated and subjected women, that has constructed human relationships into a crude and suffocating form. Why on earth should it be supported for homosexuals?"

Sullivan's 1995 book, and his most recent article, must be read in light of his 1998 testimonial *Love Undetectable: Notes on Friendship, Sex, and Survival.* This book was written after Sullivan had been diagnosed as HIV-positive. As he recalled, "I contracted the disease in full knowledge of how it is transmitted, and without any illusions about how debilitating and terrifying a diagnosis it could be. I have witnessed first-hand a man dying of AIDS; I have seen the ravages of its impact and the harrowing humiliation it meant. I had written about it, volunteered to combat it, and tried to understand it. But I still risked getting it, and the memories of that risk and the ramifications of it for myself, my family, and my friends still forced me into questions I would rather not confront, and have expended a great deal of effort avoiding."

When a high-school friend asked Sullivan how he had contracted the virus, Sullivan informed him that he had no idea which sex partner had been the source of the viral transmission. "How many people did you sleep with, for God's sake?" his friend asked. Note Sullivan's answer carefully: "Too many, God knows. Too many for meaning and dignity to be given to every one; too many for love to be present at each; too many for sex to be very often more than a temporary but powerful release from debilitating fear and loneliness." In other words, the public Andrew Sullivan emerged as a major proponent of responsibility, stability, and self-control, while the private Andrew Sullivan was deeply involved in homosexual promiscuity.

All this broke into public view in 2001, when a homosexual columnist discovered that Sullivan had been posting advertisements for unprotected homosexual sex at Internet Web sites. The ensuing controversy within the gay community was vitriolic, even as it was revealing.

"The End of Gay Culture" is an eye-opening essay. As an exercise in cultural analysis, it demonstrates genuine insight and an insider's perspective. More than anything else, Sullivan's article should awaken thinking Christians to the fact that homosexuality *is* being normalized in the larger culture. This surely represents a matter of urgent missiological concern, for the normalization of sin represents a progressive hardening of the nation's heart against the gospel.

At a more personal level, this article reminds me to

pray for Andrew Sullivan. I say this even as I realize that he may be more offended by my prayer than by anything else. In most of his writings, Sullivan demonstrates a consistent and ardent determination to celebrate homosexuality as central to his own self-discovery and personhood. Yet, he also reveals significant doubts. When he explains that he "never publicly defended promiscuity" nor publicly attacked it because "I felt, and often still feel, unable to live up to the ideals I really hold," I detect a glimmer of doubt. I have faced Mr. Sullivan in public debate on issues related to homosexuality. I consider him to be among the most gifted, thoughtful, and unpredictable intellectuals on the current scene. More than anything else, I want Mr. Sullivan to find his self-identity and deepest passions in the transforming power of Christ—the power to see all things made new. Without apology, I pray that one day he will see all that he has written in defense of homosexuality, and all that he has known in terms of his homosexual identity, as loss, and to find in Christ the only resolution of our sexuality and the only solution to the problem we *all* share—the problem of sin.

Andrew Sullivan has been a focus of my prayer since I first learned of his HIV-positive status. I do pray that God will give him strengthened health and the gift of time. After all, our Christian concern should be focused, not only on the challenge of homosexuality in the culture, but the challenge of reaching homosexuals with the love of Christ and the truth of the gospel.

14

LESBIANS RAISING SONS

Got a Problem with That?

Brian, a bright and personable third-grader, brought home from school a form that frustrated him: his family tree, complete with empty spaces for mother, father, and four spaces for grandparents. Brian's parents are a lesbian couple, his father is an unknown sperm donor. Brian's mothers worked to persuade their son that nothing was wrong with this family—instead, something was wrong with the school form."

That story was told by Peggy F. Drexler, a research psychologist and advisory board member of the San Francisco Day School. It was published in the June 16,

2004, edition of the *San Francisco Chronicle* and served notice that America is adopting "new family values." In her article, Drexler announced that she had "set out to study a new breed of mothers: lesbian couples raising sons." As a researcher, Drexler decided to focus on this population, asking a series of critical questions. Could boys thrive in a family in which there were only mothers? How would these boys develop a positive male identity and moral sense in a home where there was no father?

Drexler published her analysis in the journal *Gender and Psychoanalysis,* and she argued that sons raised in lesbian homes are "thriving." According to Drexler, boys raised by lesbian couples develop into "vibrant, courageous individuals" who are "deeply aware of their own emotional lives—including the pain that comes from discrimination against their families." Furthermore, while these boys display "all the usual traits of manliness," they also demonstrate an "openness and ease with feelings" usually associated with women. Drexler's rosy scenario, packaged as both academic research and a popular newspaper article, is evidence of efforts on the part of homosexual advocacy groups to push for the absolute normalization of homosexuality, homosexual marriage, and homosexual-led families.

Most Americans have only a minimal or abstract understanding of what this represents.

A decidedly nonabstract perspective comes in the form of *Lesbians Raising Sons,* an anthology edited by Jess Wells and published by Alyson Books of Los Angeles. The book is not new, but it has found its way into many of the nation's leading bookstore chains and local stores. Anyone still in doubt about the scale of the social revolution we are now facing should take a quick look at this book, and all will be explained.

In her introduction, Jess Wells explains that the whole issue of lesbians raising sons is due to a social and biological circumstance. Male sperm, she explains, weigh less than female sperm and therefore swim faster. Thus, in the process of artificial insemination, common among lesbians, those male sperm are more likely to reach and fertilize the egg before the female sperm. The result is that lesbian couples who undergo artificial insemination have at least a 65 percent chance of having a boy. The disproportionate number of boys born to lesbian mothers is thus, at least in part, an ironic slap in the face from an unforgiving biological fact.

Biology is one thing; parenting style is another. Lesbian mothers, Wells boasts, are raising a new generation of men who will be radically different from the boys raised in traditional "patriarchal" families. Instead of teaching boys to sublimate their emotions, to express themselves in anger and aggression, lesbians are teaching their boys "to dance, sing, decorate, play music, sew, and do theater and imaginative dress-up as well as play football and baseball, surf, ski, and shoot hoops."

In the short span of this introductory essay, Wells presents lesbians mothering sons as revolutionaries ready to overthrow a patriarchal social order. "The right wing reacts to lesbian mothers with a vengeance for several reasons," Wells laments. "We procreate without intercourse; we raise sons without men in the house; and we teach boys not to oppress women, to feel, and to live free of gender restrictions and homophobia." *Lesbians Raising Sons* includes thirty-six additional chapters, all dealing with different dimensions of lesbian motherhood and sons. In her article, Peggy Drexler had argued that the ability to grow into manhood is innate in boys, and that based on her "research," boys do not need a male role-model in the home to teach them how to be men.

Perhaps she should have read *Lesbians Raising Sons*. If so, she would have encountered a very different line of argument and evidence. In the book's first chapter,

Sara Asch wrote of her son, "who is apparently a girl and who, if he were old enough to read this, would be furious at me for using this male pronoun." She goes on to explain that the boy wears eleven braids decorated with eighty-eight beads. "Flowing tresses is the effect he seeks…. He knows how to toss his head just so, to tuck a lock behind his ear, to suck on a strand that reaches the mouth."

So much for "all the usual traits of manliness." Robin Morgan, writing of her own experience mothering a son, recalled that her son's earliest bedtime stories featured strong, heroic women and "gentle" men. According to Morgan, she and her partner made up the stories themselves "because there were almost no antisexist children's books then available." She also related that her son was very rarely disciplined or punished in any way. "Instead, we'd talk about it," she said. She also relates that her son, now grown, reflects, "I almost longed to be simply forbidden something or punished for something, like other kids."

Morgan and her partner also worked to create a feminist environment in which their son would be raised. "We tried to offer alternatives to the patriarchal 'norms.'… He was offered—and played with—dolls and tea sets as well as with fire trucks and tractors."

An even more extreme vision of lesbian mother-hood and sons was related by Ruthann Robson as she explained the response of lesbian separatists to the birth of her son. Having been separatists themselves, they were puzzled by how they would deal with this baby boy. "What were two dykes going to do with this minia-ture emissary from the patriarchy who invaded our lives?" Robson defines lesbian separatism as a lifestyle in which lesbians "devote their considerable energies, inso-far as it is possible, exclusively to other lesbians or, in some cases, exclusively to other women." Clearly, the birth of a boy ruins this women-only picture.

When Colby, Robson's son, was born, she even feared that her lesbian partner would leave her. "I kept thinking of all the concerts from which we'd be ex-cluded, all the radical conferences at which we wouldn't be welcome, all the women's land on which we could never live."

What happened? Robson tells that their friends largely left them. "Inez said she could no longer come to meetings at our house because our rooms exuded maleness." Raquel, another friend, "told us she couldn't believe we simply didn't give up the 'male child' for adoption." Another lesbian friend showed up to give speeches "about lesbian strength being dissipated, about lesbian separatist ethics, about lesbian obligations to the future, about the inviolability of gender." Finally, another lesbian, whose sexual advances Robson had rejected, "stood up at the Coconut Grove Lesbian Dance, Meeting, and Pot Luck and proposed a rule that would bar all 'lesbians in any way participating in male-energized households' from the group."

In her own chapter, Jess Wells insisted that she had done everything within her power to avoid giving birth to a son. "How had this happened? I had paid to have the sperm sex-selected. The sperm had been made to swim for hours, and the fastest swimmers—the 'male' sperm—had been poured down the sink.... I had been planning on a girl," Wells remembered. "It was essential that I have a girl." When she was told that her womb contained a boy, she was "profoundly disappointed." As an ardent opponent of "male privilege, patriarchy, and male culture," Wells didn't want anything to do with raising a boy. Eventually, she was reconciled to the fact that her child was a boy and decided this could be a positive experience. "My son cannot take me away from the struggle for women's rights, nor can he force me to take an interest in anything that I don't deem interesting. He cannot be my oppressor because he is my child, and he cannot be a second chance to relive my life because he has his own life. He and I will explore each other's cultures, sharing what we can and respecting what we can't.... Both of us, respecting each other's sovereignty, can rejoice in our foreignness and celebrate our diversity."

The prophets of political correctness now tell us that diversity is the order of the day, and that "diverse forms of family" are to be greeted with enthusiasm. Those who insist that marriage is the union of a man and a woman and that parenthood should flow from that union are now dismissed as intolerant, closed-minded extremists. Even in the face of such intimidation, a quick look at *Lesbians Raising Sons* should be sufficient to help the vast majority of Americans know who the real extremists are.

15

THE AGE OF POLYMORPHOUS PERVERSITY

A Revolution Fueled by Ideas

The sexual issues now confronting our nation—from the breakdown of the family to same-sex marriage—are really pieces of a much larger puzzle. In order to understand what is happening, one must look carefully at the entire picture, the entire trajectory of Western civilization over the past century. What we face today are not individual, isolated issues but rather a massive social transformation that has not happened by accident and that will not break apart on its own.

In the early 1930s, the esteemed historian Christopher Dawson wrote, "Western civilization at the present day is passing through a crisis which is essentially different from anything that has previously been experienced. Other societies in the past have changed their social institutions or their religious beliefs under the influence of external forces or the slow development of internal growth. But none, like our own, has ever consciously faced the prospect of a fundamental alteration of the beliefs and institutions on which the whole fabric of social life rests."[1]

From the vantage point of 1930, Dawson looked forward to the rest of the twentieth century, and he understood what was happening. He was a prophet.

In order to understand the shift that Dawson foresaw and that ultimately took place, it is necessary to look back to 1909, when Sigmund Freud released his understanding of human sexuality. Trying to understand something as powerful as sex, Freud turned to what he called the "infantile" stage of human development, identifying the leading characteristic of infantile sexuality as *polymorphous perversity.* Freud explained: What makes an infant characteristically different from

---

1. Christopher Dawson, *Enquiries into Religion and Culture* (New York: Sheed & Ward, 1933).

every other stage of human life is that the child is "polymorphously perverse," meaning that the infant is ready to demonstrate any kind of sexual behavior without any kind of restraint.[2] He then explained how "civilization" emerges only after this innate, polymorphous perversity is restrained by psychological repression, social form, and custom. Such restraint, Freud felt, was inevitable and indeed necessary, for procreation is necessary for the continuation of the race, and therefore heterosexual coupling was absolutely essential for civilization itself. Even if we finally reject Freud's theory, it is crucial that we understand its influence. Freud is no doubt one of the ideological horsemen of the twentieth-century apocalypse, but even he was outdone by those who came after him.

In the second half of the twentieth century, Herbert Marcuse revisited Freud in his book *Eros and Civilization,* mixing his theories with those of Marx in order to develop a theory of sexuality as liberation.[3] The whole problem, Marcuse thought, was the very restraint that Freud believed was inevitable and necessary, the

2. Sigmund Freud, *Three Contributions to the Theory of Sex* in *The Basic Writings of Sigmund Freud,* trans. A. A. Brill, (New York: Modern Library, 1995).

3. Herbert Marcuse, *Eros and Civilization: A Philosophical Inquiry into Freud* (Boston: Beacon, 1955).

repression that Freud saw leading to civilization itself. According to Marcuse, the only way to achieve liberation is to undo that repression, reverse that restraint, and thus unleash in society itself that infantile stage of pure sexuality—of polymorphous perversity.

In the 1960s, *Eros and Civilization* received much attention on college campuses, where such ideas are always met with an enthusiastic audience. But the rest of the culture remained largely unaware of, and untroubled by, the assault that had begun to take place upon the very foundations of civilization itself. Now it has become obvious that this ideology of polymorphous perversity is inch by inch—if not yard by yard—gaining ground. Read the daily newspaper, or just review the events of a typical week. Even something as basic as the heterosexual nature of marriage is now very much under assault. The very idea of normality, or of fixed institutions, is being subverted by the culture and marginalized by cultural elites. What we now face is the subversion of humanity's most basic categories and institutions—gender, marriage, and family. In the eyes of all too many in our culture, gender is merely a plastic social construct. Indeed, in the postmodern world, all realities are plastic and all principles are liquid. Everything can be changed. Nothing is fixed. All truth is relative, all truth is socially constructed, and anything that is constructed can also be deconstructed in order to liberate.

We are now told that even gender should be seen as a continuum. This means that human beings are no longer categorized as male and female but as any number of chosen gender options. Furthermore, gender is flexible, at least according to the postmodern prophets of liberation. You can always change your gender if you do not like the gender you were assigned at birth. Interestingly, some surgeons are now even reversing gender transformation surgeries they had earlier performed. All this represents a denial of gender as a part of the goodness of God's creation. According to the biblical account of creation, human beings were created as male and female, and these categories establish the very basis for human order. This is now dismissed as inherently oppressive and intolerant.

For years, the ideological elites have believed that marriage is repressive and inhibiting. It is, they say, merely a product of social evolution, an institution that developed because civilization needed a way to protect children and to encourage child rearing. But of course, that which has evolved can always evolve further, and the next step, we are told, is to move beyond marriage altogether. This was the goal of the cultural elites in the latter half of the twentieth century, and we must admit that they have made great strides toward accomplishing their objective.

If any one institution in human life was most subverted in the twentieth century, it was without doubt the institution of marriage. Assaulted by divorce, lifestyle, media, law, politics, and custom, marriage was undermined in its very essence. Of course, the attack also necessarily took its toll on the family as well. The very idea of the family as a fixed unit—a husband and wife and their children, together with their extended family—is now seen as an archaic, antiquarian, and intolerant institution, one which must be undone so that humanity may be liberated from oppression.

Revolutions are fueled by ideas. The cultural upheaval represented by the age of polymorphous perversity has been grounded primarily in the ideas of three individuals: Margaret Mead, Alfred Kinsey, and Michel Foucault. To understand the force and speed with which this philosophy of polymorphous perversity has impacted and changed the culture, one must first understand the ideas that undergird it.

Margaret Mead is considered one of the founders of anthropology in America. After a research visit to the Pacific islands, Mead wrote a book in 1928 entitled *Coming of Age in Samoa.* The book, which essentially launched Mead's career as an anthropologist, argued that Samoan adolescence—unlike Western adolescence— was a time of smooth transition from childhood to adulthood because Samoans tended to enjoy casual sex for many years before they settled into marriage. The bottom line, according to Mead, was that promiscuity is healthy. History has proven, however, that Mead was a fraud. Her entire project was based on falsehood and misinformation. Five years after Mead's death in 1978, Derek Freeman published a book entitled *Margaret Mead and Samoa: The Making and Unmaking of an Anthropological Myth,* in which he challenged and re-futed every one of Mead's major claims. Returning to Samoa to question the actual subjects of Mead's re-search, he found that the young women to whom Mead had spoken had simply lied to her about their promiscuity. Even so, the book had an enormous influence on American culture and attitudes toward sex and marriage for more than fifty years.

Another intellectual engine of the age of polymorphous perversity is Alfred Kinsey. Quite frankly, Kinsey was one of the most influential sexual deviants of the twentieth century. In fact, he stands as a symbol of everything that went wrong during that period. His book *Sexual Behavior in the Human Male,* published in 1948, prompted a revolution by providing a pseudoscientific cover to those who were pushing the age of polymorphous perversity. Kinsey simply pushed Margaret Mead's conclusion one step further. If Mead taught that promiscuity is healthy, Kinsey argued that perversity itself is healthy. Sexual deviance is simply to be celebrated.

Finally, we turn to consider Michel Foucault. Probably the least well known of this trio, Foucault was a dominant influence in the American academy—a French philosopher who died after being infected with AIDS in the gay bars of San Francisco, California. Foucault, one of the dominant figures in postmodern thought, taught that sex is everything and that the only way to be liberated is to sexualize every dimension of life in the direction of polymorphous perversity. In essence, Foucault argued that sexuality is itself a modern invention and that one of modern society's central ambitions has been to institutionalize sexual repression. Though he died in 1984, Foucault is undoubtedly still one of the most influential persons on American college campuses today.

Fueled by the ideas of Margaret Mead, Alfred Kinsey, and Michel Foucault, this age of polymorphous perversity is now upon us. The subversion of marriage and the family has extended to law and morality, to authority and to custom. The very habits of human life—the customs and traditions on which civilization is grounded—are now being reversed, marginalized, and discarded in an effort to eliminate all norms by normalizing the abnormal. For those whose agenda is to undermine Judeo-Christian morality and to disconnect Western civilization from biblical norms, there is no better strategy than to subvert marriage, family, and sexuality, unleashing on society an age and culture of polymorphous perversity.

16

THE AGE OF POLYMORPHOUS PERVERSITY

Seven Strategies for Revolution

The massive social transformation that is now taking place in America—the jettisoning of tradition, the overthrowing of fixed institutions, the normalizing of the abnormal; in short, the establishment of a new age and culture of polymorphous perversity—has not come about by accident. It is the result of a comprehensive strategy intended to change the way people think at every conceivable level.

First, there is a *psychological strategy.* We live in a therapeutic age in which every movement must be presented within a psychological framework. The strategy of those who push the agenda of polymorphous perversity has been to define sexuality as merely a matter of self-conscious orientation. When the question is changed from what individuals *do* to what individuals *are* as a psychological construct, the moral equation is absolutely transformed. The idea that personal autonomy is at the very core of what it means to be human is now ubiquitous in the therapeutic culture, and thus the most important realities have become autonomy, self-esteem, and self-actualization. Anything that represses the uninhibited demonstration of the inner yearnings of the self is considered unhealthy and repressive, and should therefore be illegal and even immoral, marginalized, and eradicated.

Second, there is a *medical strategy.* Anything that can be "psychologized" can also be "medicalized." In 1973, the American Psychiatric Association (APA) voted to remove homosexuality from the *Diagnostic and Statistical Manual of Mental Disorders,* the organization's official list of mental illnesses. In other words, on one day homosexuality was considered to be a mental disorder, and on the next day it was not. But of course this is medicine based on ideology rather than on science. The decision by the APA to normalize homosexuality did not come as a result of unquestioned scientific studies, nor because someone in a laboratory suddenly discovered that homosexuality was in fact normal. To the contrary, the APA's decision came because special-interest groups forced the change upon them, and the physicians willingly surrendered.

Do not underestimate the significance of that decision. It is not merely that homosexuality was considered aberrant in one moment and normal in the next. It is that *believing* homosexuality to be wrong and aberrant was normal and acceptable in one moment but a symptom of mental illness and bigotry in the next. This was a complete moral revolution, and yet it went unnoticed by most Americans. We now face a new concept of "normal" that has been foisted upon society by medical authorities and that has brought about a great reversal in moral thinking. The belief that heterosexuality is normative, once a sign of healthy and stable moral thinking, is now seen to be unhealthy and repressive. On the other hand, homosexuality, once considered unhealthy and wrong, is now accepted as a perfectly legitimate "alternative lifestyle."

Not only is there a psychological strategy and a

medical strategy, but there is also a *political strategy*. The late twentieth century saw the development of special-interest politics, in which every group with a special agenda formed itself into an organization, hired lobbyists, and went at the political process with gusto. Protest was the first step, and political action was its aftermath.

When we think about this political strategy, we must raise an interesting question—just how successful has it been? Amazingly, of all the strategies we will discuss, this political strategy has actually been the *least* effective for the homosexual movement and for the age of polymorphous perversity as a whole. Why? Because the American people simply are not buying it. Americans are often asleep as fundamental changes are taking place, but when they face an actual choice at the ballot box, overwhelmingly they tend to choose to normalize the *normal* rather than the abnormal. Think about the numerous different constitutional amendments passed by various states in the last few elections, identifying marriage as the union of one man and one woman. Americans' instinctive reflex to normalize the normal explains why the proponents of polymorphous perversity have been so frustrated in the political realm.

Of course, with the failure of the political strategy

to deliver a satisfactory outcome, the age of polymorphous perversity has leaned largely upon a *legal strategy*. This was made possible by the judicial usurpation of politics. As former judge Robert Bork has so prophetically stated, we now face a tyranny of judges with an ideology of judicial activism, who treat the law as a playground for social innovation, social revolution, and ideological subversion. Harvard Law School professor Mary Ann Glendon's observation about the ascendancy of "rights talk" is also instructive. Everything is about rights. Right and wrong no longer have any meaning as categories in the law. According to the critical legal theory now being taught in law schools, there is no right or wrong, only competing rights. And of course, many of these rights are invented rights, supposedly discovered in the "penumbras and emanations" of the United States Constitution.

This legal strategy has been extremely effective. From the 1973 *Roe v. Wade* decision to the *Lawrence v. Texas* decision of 2003, the Supreme Court has been a willing accomplice of the Left in bringing about social and moral revolution. In his scathing dissent from the majority's opinion in *Lawrence v. Texas,* Justice Antonin Scalia said that the decision amounted to nothing less than the end of all morals legislation in the United

States of America. Given the specific arguments Justice
Anthony Kennedy made in the majority opinion, no
legislation based on morality would ever pass constitutional muster again. In one decision in the year 2003,
the United States Supreme Court swept morality off
the table of America's public life.

Besides the psychological, medical, political, and
legal strategies, there is also an *educational strategy* directed at the schools and at the young. The goal here is
to reach the young and ultimately to separate them
from their parents, freeing them from parental authority and parental teaching. Earlier in the twentieth century, it was John Dewey who first argued that society
ought to act decisively to free children from the repressive prejudices of their parents. His philosophy largely
won the day, and that is where we now stand. Elementary schools have essentially become laboratories of
social engineering. In fact, groups like the Gay, Lesbian,
and Straight Education Network have mobilized to influence the curricula of the schools with the goal of
changing young minds. By introducing their programs,
literature, and media into elementary school class-
rooms, they hope and intend to infect the next generation with this ideology of polymorphous perversity.

Take a look at the artwork now found in elementary school textbooks. Look at who is holding hands. Look at who is embracing. The nuclear family—Mom, Dad, Dick, and Jane—is no longer to be taken for granted. If the agents of polymorphous perversity have their way, Dick and Jane will now be raised with two moms, or two dads, or any other conceivable "family arrangement." The important thing is for children to be disabused of the notion—brought on by their parents' irrational prejudices—that marriage and family are somehow normatively heterosexual.

This strategy is only accelerated in middle and high schools. There, the ideological induction is radically increased with mechanisms such as comprehensive sex education. *Comprehensive,* of course, does not refer to a deeper understanding of the nature of human sexuality. Nor does it point to a deeper comprehension of the moral issues at stake. Sex education is *comprehensive* only in the sense that nothing is deemed out of bounds, including sexual technique and contraceptive advice. Morally, anything goes—so long as it is personally fulfilling.

School-based clinics are another tool of the age of polymorphous perversity. Once again, children are separated from the authority and teaching of their parents and shuffled off to clinics where they are offered all manner of "assistance"—from sexual counseling to contraceptives. Often this happens without any parental knowledge at all, much less parental notification or permission. Other special programs are directed to middle- and high-school students in such a way that most parents have no idea what their children are actually learning. Rarely do these events have the word *sex* in them, and only by mistake are they ever packaged in such a way as to trigger parents' concern. Instead, they are advertised as "special emphasis weeks" focusing on diversity, tolerance, and difference.

Even textbooks reflect these changes. The agents of polymorphous perversity have made public school curricula the objects of their strategic concern, and it is increasingly common for teenagers and even younger children to read books categorized under "young adult literature." Many of these books are nothing less than pornographic. They are evangelistic tracts for the age of polymorphous perversity, and they have found their way even onto the shelves of many school libraries.

The college and university level, for its part, is now a circus of sexual revolution. Considering this, author Paul Berman once said, "It is now forbidden anymore to forbid." But the revolution is not strictly from the bottom up. It is also being pressed from the top down, with increasing numbers of colleges and universities even offering programs in gay and lesbian studies. All this is an ideological engine for placing within the university structure, within the faculty, and within the curriculum a seed of sexual revolution that will ultimately normalize the abnormal and abnormalize the normal. Furthermore, anyone who is not "with it" is not only sick and pitiable but is in fact dangerous to the body politic—backward, ignorant, and repressive.

This has led in many university cultures to a specific targeting of Christian organizations. At places like Tufts University, the University of North Carolina at Chapel Hill, and some Ivy League institutions, there have been cases in which Christian organizations have been told that they must allow practicing homosexuals to be officers in their organizations or they will be barred from campus and removed from recognition as an official student group. In other words, a Christian organization may remain on campus only so long as it forfeits Christian morality, all in the name of diversity and tolerance.

There is also a *cultural strategy* focused on the elite centers of American culture. The media industry, the entertainment industry, music, and even advertising have essentially become the bulletin-board dissemination service for the age of polymorphous perversity. Many Christians would be shocked to see how some

companies who carefully manage their wholesome images advertise to the homosexual community. Many of
these are corporations whose names we know and
whose products we buy, but they present an entirely
different face when extending themselves to the culture
of polymorphous perversity.

It is no exaggeration to note that Hollywood, with
very rare exceptions, is simply given over to this culture. In fact, Hollywood's movies have become the
principal means whereby the culture of polymorphous
perversity is mainstreamed to the entire nation. So
even though it might appear from electoral maps that
this polymorphous perversity is confined to the coasts
and a few other urban areas, the reality is that this philosophy of liberation reaches into every community
and into every home by means of entertainment,
music, movies, and advertising.

Finally, there is a *theological strategy.* The single
greatest obstacle to the victory of the culture of polymorphous perversity is the Judeo-Christian heritage.
The greatest obstacle to the normalization of homosexuality is the Bible. Therefore, the cultural revolutionaries have implemented a strategy to completely transform
the understanding of sexuality as handed down in the
Scriptures and as understood by the Christian church

throughout the centuries. What has emerged from this subversion of theology is two rival traditions, two religions, each claiming to be Christian. One of these "Christianities" is no longer based upon biblical authority, no longer committed to the great doctrines of the faith, and no longer committed to the faith once for all delivered to the saints. Yet it continues to bear the name "Christian" and continues to claim that its adherents have not in fact abandoned the authority of Scripture.

The sin of Sodom and Gomorrah, they claim, was not homosexuality, but *inhospitality*. This, however, is a recklessly subversive argument. It simply ignores the clear import of the story in favor of advancing a cause. What about those passages in Leviticus that condemn homosexual acts? What they suggest, according to the cultural revolutionaries, is that homosexual acts are sinful only insofar as they are specifically committed by persons who are heterosexual. A similar argument is made about Paul's reasoning in Romans 1. Paul had no understanding of our modern idea of sexual orientation, the argument goes. Nevertheless, his teachings are still useful because they remind us that a person should follow his or her orientation: to violate one's sexual orientation would be a sin against nature—not nature itself, but one's *own* nature.

Yet it seems clear from Romans 1 that the apostle Paul had a pretty good idea of sexual orientation. In fact, Paul very clearly indicts sinful sexual orientation, for he deals not only with sexual *activity* but with the *passions* that lead to such activity. "Men," he says, "abandoned the natural function of the woman and burned in their desire toward one another" (verse 27). The Bible simply leaves no room for equivocation.

As the late Elizabeth Achtemeier of Union Theological Seminary once argued, if there is any one thing that is plainly revealed in Scripture, it is Scripture's absolute condemnation of homosexuality in every form and in every context. There is no room for negotiation. If homosexuality is to be squared with biblical teaching, it will only be through subverting the entire authority of Scripture and by setting up a rival version of Christianity.

In all these areas—psychological, medical, political, legal, educational, cultural, and even theological—the age of polymorphous perversity has made great strides toward entrenching itself in the Western mind. The great question is whether our civilization can survive this assault. And the answer, of course, is no—not unless there is a fast recovery of the biblical worldview.

17

THE AGE OF POLYMORPHOUS PERVERSITY

Can Civilization Survive?

M oral relativism is the order of the day, and it all begs the question "Can civilization survive?" The answer is, quite simply, no. Civilization cannot survive the triumph of the age of polymorphous perversity, because the idea of polymorphous sex is hopelessly incompatible with the very notion of civilization itself. Civilization is based upon order, respect, habit, custom, and institution—all of which are rejected outright by the age of polymorphous perversity.

Looking at the history of Western civilization, William and Ariel Durant argued that one of the first achievements necessary for the establishment of civilization is the restraint of sexuality. As they put it, sexuality is like a hot river that must be banked on both sides. Sadly, what we see in the latter half of the twentieth century is the unbanking of that river.[1]

Pitirim A. Sorokin, founder of the department of sociology at Harvard University, argued that heterosexual marriage is the foundation of civilization itself. You simply cannot build or maintain civilization without heterosexual marriage, and without heterosexual marriage being understood as the norm. Unless heterosexual marriage is protected by law, custom, and habit to the exclusion of every other arrangement, civilization is impossible. Sorokin made this point more than fifty years ago. Even from such a distance, he saw this age of perversity arising, and he argued that this age of rebellion would destroy civilization. Yet he also held out the hope that civilization would wake up when the issue finally came down to the preservation of marriage. Was he right?

---

1. William and Ariel Durant, *The Lessons of History* (New York: Simon and Schuster, 1968), 35.

That is the great question of our day—whether or not this civilization will indeed wake up once marriage is clearly understood to be *the* critical battleground and *the* primary target of attack. Today, we face a cultural crisis that actually threatens to reverse civilization and to embrace barbarism. Can civilization survive under these circumstances? I would have to argue that it cannot. There is no example in the history of humankind of a civilization enduring for long when an age of polymorphous perversity is set loose.

Can we recover from this? We certainly must hope and pray so, but any recovery will have to be based on a re-embrace of biblical truth. We simply will not find enough sociological capital to reverse the prevailing trends. We will not find enough legal conviction to withstand this assault from cultural revolutionaries. Nor will we find enough political momentum to halt this movement. In the end, there is only one thing that stands between this culture and absolute dissolution, and that is the fact that sex was not our idea. Human beings are creatures made by a sovereign Creator, who made us male and female for His glory and who created the institution of marriage both for our health and for our happiness.

As J. R. R. Tolkien once said to his son Michael,

"You must remember, son, that monogamy is a revealed ethic." No one accidentally stumbles across monogamy, and this culture will not stumble onto recovery. It will have to submit itself to recovery. What is needed is a spiritual, theological, and biblical recovery, one that sees gender not as some kind of evolutionary accident but as God's gift, part of the very goodness of God's creation. We see God's glory in the masculinity of the male and in the femininity of the female. We understand gender to be a fixed category, not an accidental aberration in the evolutionary process of humanity. Given this, we must remind the culture that marriage is not merely a social contract between two (or more) people but an arena in which the glory of God is displayed in the right ordering of one man and one woman who come together in the permanent, holy covenant of marriage.

We must refuse to separate the goods of marriage, and we must again point out that part of the essential function of marriage is procreation. Those who are able to have children must welcome children, because this is what God has instituted. Sex, procreation, marriage, and family must be woven together in a seamless garment that recognizes children as a divine gift. In this family—man, woman, and children—civilization is enriched and strengthened, and even more importantly, God's glory is evident in the midst of His creation.

What then are we to do in order to work for recovery from this age of polymorphous perversity? First, we must fight on every front. We must fight on the legal front, the political front, the media front, the cultural front, the educational front, the psychological front, and the medical front. In each of these crucial arenas, we must bear witness to the truth. In doing so, we may be marginalized, we may be voted down, and we may be criticized, but we cannot simply surrender the field to the other side.

Second, we must bear witness to the truth. This means that we must be very careful not only to *say* the right things but also to *show* the right things. In other words, we must make certain that our marriages and our families are a testimony to God's intention, and that we live before the world declaring that even if insanity, irrationality, and sexual anarchy rule the world, it will not rule us. God's glory will be shown in faithfulness wherever it is found, even in the tiny domestic picture of our seemingly insignificant families. The age of polymorphous perversity may one day become the rule of the land. The cultural revolutionaries may one day be successful beyond their wildest dreams. But so long as there remains one man and one woman united in holy marriage, receiving children as God's gifts and ordering their family life by the Word of God, there will still be a powerful witness that the world cannot ignore.

Third, we must create communities of faithful marriages and healthy families. Our churches must become communities that demonstrate the wonder of God's glory in marriage and the holiness of God's intention in sex. We must band ourselves together so that we live this witness before the world and train our children to do the same.

Fourth, we must rescue the perishing and love the unlovely. What happens when those who give themselves to the culture of polymorphous perversity finally get sick or collapse in despair? The church of the Lord Jesus Christ is made up of sinners saved by grace—sinners who understand what sin is and who understand that Jesus Christ came to save sinners. Thus, we must be about the task of rescuing the perishing and loving the unlovely, for so also, in our own way, were we.

Let us then see this trend toward sexual anarchy answered with true resolve. Let us mount a movement, not consisting so much of placards, billboards, and advertising, but of couples and families, men and women who will not bend, will not bow, and will not surrender to the culture of polymorphous perversity.

Inform Your Faith

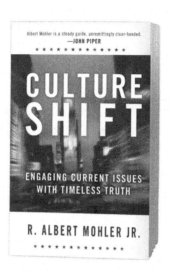

Dr. Mohler addresses tough issues clearly, biblically, and passionately. Topics include Christian faith and politics, public schools, terrorism, abortion, The Supreme Court and religion, and many more.

Combat moral relativism.

Get informed.

Stand up for the truth.

Arm yourself for the battle...pick up a copy from your favorite bookstore or online retailer!

www.albertmohler.com

More Resources from
R. Albert Mohler, Jr.!

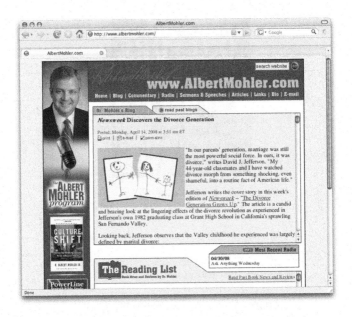

For blogs on current issues, sermons and speeches, articles and more, please visit Dr. Mohler's website at www.albertmohler.com. Also available - information on the Albert Mohler Radio Program.

Printed in the United States
by Baker & Taylor Publisher Services